DISCARDED

Documents on British Policy Overseas, Series III, Vol. VI

This volume consists of a book and fully searchable DVD containing a facsimile collection of diplomatic documents covering British reactions to critical developments regarding Berlin, its quadripartite administration, and role in the Cold War during the periods 1948–49, 1959–61 and 1988–90.

The developments thus documented are each set within very different international contexts, but four interrelated themes are nevertheless common to each of the three chapters of the volume: the British Government's insistence, in conjunction with the Americans and the French, on upholding and safeguarding the rights of the four occupying powers in Berlin; British concerns with broader matters of military security in Western Europe as a whole and Germany in particular; the interaction of the four occupying powers with one another; and the questions raised by demographic change, especially population movements from east to west. All of the documents dealing with the events of 1988–90 fall within the UK's 30-year rule and have therefore not hitherto been in the public domain.

This volume will be of great interest to students of International History, British Political History, and European Politics and International Relations in general.

Keith Hamilton is Consultant Historian at the Foreign and Commonwealth Office and Senior Editor of *Documents on British Policy Overseas.*

Patrick Salmon is Chief Historian at the Foreign and Commonwealth Office.

Stephen Twigge is Senior Historian at the Foreign and Commonwealth Office.

Whitehall Histories: Foreign and Commonwealth Office Publications

Series Editors: Keith Hamilton and Patrick Salmon

ISSN: 1471–2083

FCO historians are responsible for editing *Documents on British Policy Overseas (DBPO)* and for overseeing the publication of FCO Internal Histories.

DBPO comprises three series of diplomatic documents, focusing on major themes in foreign policy since 1945, and drawn principally from the records of the Foreign and Commonwealth Office. The latest volumes, published in Series III, are composed almost wholly of documents from within the thirty-year 'closed period', which would otherwise be unavailable to the public.

FCO Internal Histories are occasional studies by former serving officials, commissioned to provide background information for members of the FCO, to point out possible lessons for the future and to evaluate how well objectives were met in a particular episode or crisis. They are not written for publication, but some Internal Histories, which offer fresh insights into British diplomacy, are now being declassified for publication by Whitehall History Publishing in association with Routledge.

Latest published volumes:

Britain and China, 1945–1950
Documents on British Policy Overseas, Series I, Volume VIII
S.R. Ashton, G. Bennett and K. A. Hamilton (eds)

Britain and the Soviet Union, 1968–1972
Documents on British Policy Overseas, Series III, Volume I
G. Bennett and K.A. Hamilton (eds)

The Conference on Security and Cooperation in Europe, 1972–1975
Documents on British Policy Overseas, Series III, Volume II
G. Bennett and K.A. Hamilton (eds)

Détente in Europe, 1972–1976
Documents on British Policy Overseas, Series III, Volume III
G. Bennett and K.A. Hamilton (eds)

The Year of Europe: America, Europe and the Energy Crisis, 1972–1974
Documents on British Policy Overseas, Series III, Volume IV
K.A. Hamilton and P. Salmon (eds)

The Southern Flank in Crisis, 1973–1976
Documents on British Policy Overseas, Series III, Volume V
K.A. Hamilton and P. Salmon (eds)

Berlin in the Cold War, 1948–1990
Documents on British Policy Overseas, Series III, Volume VI
K.A. Hamilton, P. Salmon and S. Twigge (eds)

Documents on British Policy Overseas, Series III, Vol. VI

Berlin in the Cold War, 1948–1990

Edited by Keith Hamilton,
Patrick Salmon and Stephen Twigge

LONDON AND NEW YORK

First published 2009
by Routledge
2 Park Square, Milton Park, Abingdon, Oxon OX14 4RN

Simultaneously published in the USA and Canada
by Routledge
270 Madison Avenue, New York, NY 10016

Routledge is an imprint of the Taylor & Francis Group, an informa business

Publisher's note
This book has been prepared from a camera-ready copy supplied by the editors

Printed and bound in Great Britain by
TJI Digital, Padstow, Cornwall

British Library Cataloguing in Publication Data
A catalogue record for this book is available from the British Library

Library of Congress Cataloging in Publication Data
A catalog record has been requested for this book

ISBN10: 0–415–44870–0
ISBN13: 978–0–415–44870–3

CONTENTS

		PAGES
Abbreviations		1-6
List of Persons		7-44
Introductions and Summaries		
Chapter I	Berlin Isolated, 1948-49	45-74
Chapter II	Berlin Divided, 1959-61	75-96
Chapter III	Berlin Reunited, 1988-90	97-119

DVD

The DVD should auto-start. If it does not, follow the instructions below:

- Open 'My Computer'
- Read the drive for your DVD player
- Locate file 'Berlin.pdf' and double-click

Documents can be accessed by clicking on the entries in the Document Summaries.

To navigate between documents, it is recommended that the reader open the 'bookmarks' tab and then expand each heading by clicking on the + box.

System Requirements:

- Adobe Reader 6.0 or higher – can be downloaded free if charge from the Adobe website *www.adobe.co.uk* or via the Help menu in your current Adobe Reader.

PREFACE

This is the second volume of *Documents on British Policy Overseas* (DBPO) to be published in electronic format. As in the case of the previous volume, *The Year of Europe: America, Europe and the Energy Crisis, 1972-1974*, the documents, some 509 in all, appear in facsimile on an accompanying disc, and brief summaries of their contents are here reproduced in printed text, along with historical introductions and lists of abbreviations and persons. However, this volume breaks with previous practice in style and composition. Its documentation is not limited to a single chronological period, but extends over three narrowly defined and widely separated moments of Cold War history. Ms Gill Bennett, the former Chief Historian of the Foreign and Commonwealth Office (FCO), who was responsible for the selection, conceived of a volume which would focus upon British policy towards Berlin during 1948-49, 1959-61 and 1989-90, years which highlighted the significance of Germany's divided and occupied capital both as a source and a measure of East-West tensions in Europe. The Berlin airlift, the building of the Berlin wall, and finally its demolition twenty-eight years later, gave material meaning to a global contest often otherwise perceived in terms of ideology and superpower rivalry.

These events were, as described in the introductions to the document summaries, set within very different international contexts. Britain's diplomatic involvement with them was also conditioned by the emergence of two German states and the creation and consolidation of the Atlantic Alliance. Four interrelated themes are nevertheless common to each of the three chapters of the volume: the British Government's insistence, in conjunction with the Americans and the French, on upholding and safeguarding the rights of the four occupying powers in Berlin; British concerns with broader matters of military security in Western Europe as a whole and Germany in particular; the interaction of the four occupying powers with each other; and the questions raised by demographic change, especially population movements from east to west. Human rights, individual liberties and the well-being of families as well as nations, were inextricably bound up with high politics and grand strategy when it came to framing policies on Berlin.

Acknowledgements

In accordance with the Parliamentary announcement cited in the Introduction to the Series, the Editors have had the customary freedom in the selection and arrangement of documents including full access to all classes of FCO documentation. There have, in the case of the present volume, been no exceptional cases, such as were provided for in the Parliamentary announcement, where it has been necessary on security grounds to restrict the availability of particular documents, editorially selected in accordance with regular practice.

The main source of documentation in this volume has been the records of the Foreign Office, and its successor Department, the Foreign and Commonwealth Office, including those currently held by the FCO's Information Management Group (IMG), pending their transfer to The National Archives. For their help in providing access to these archives and locating specific files we are grateful to Ms Jane Darby, the Head of IMG, and her staff, particularly the Records Retrieval Team at Hanslope Park. We are also indebted to the staff of what was formerly FCO Library Information Services for their aid with printed sources; to the Histories, Openness and Records Unit of the Cabinet Office for facilitating our researches; to Mr Tony Bishop and Mr Bob Dixon for their historical advice; to Dr

Alastair Noble for his editorial support; and to Mr Andrew Plummer-Rodriguez, Mr Grant Hibberd, Mr Giles Rose and Dr Isabelle Tombs for their research and technical input. Special thanks are, however, due to Ms Bennett, whose project this initially was; to Dr Nigel Jarvis, formerly of FCO Historians, who first assisted her with the selection of documents; and to Dr Christopher Baxter, now of Queen's University, Belfast, who oversaw much of the later work on the volume.

KEITH HAMILTON
PATRICK SALMON
STEPHEN TWIGGE

June 2008

ABBREVIATIONS

AA	*Auswärtiges Amt*/Federal German Foreign Ministry
ABC	American Broadcasting Company
ACA	Allied Control Authority
ACC	Allied Control Council
ACDD	Arms Control and Disarmament Department, FCO
ACDS	Assistant Chief of the Defence Staff
ACGS	Assistant Chief of the General Staff
ADAC	Allgemeiner Deutscher Automobile-Club
ADIZ	Air Defence Identification Zone
ADN	*Allgemeiner Deutscher Nachrichtendienst*/General German (GDR state-controlled) News Service
AF	Air France
AFCENT	Allied Forces Central Europe (NATO)
AK	Allied *Kommandatura*, Berlin
AL	*Alternative Liste*/Alternative List (for Democracy and Protection of the Environment)
AMB	Allied Mediation Bureau
AMD	Aviation and Maritime Department, FCO
APS	Assistant Private Secretary
ATC	Air Traffic Control
ATO	Allied Travel Office
ATP	Advanced Turboprop (British Aerospace airliner)
ATS	Auxilliary Territorial Service
AUS	Assistant Under-Secretary of State
BA	British Airways
BAA	British Airports Authority
BAFO	British Air Forces of Occupation
BAOR	British Army of the Rhine
BARTCC	Berlin Air Route Traffic Coordination Centre
BASC	Berlin Air Safety Centre
BBC	British Broadcasting Corporation
BCATAG	Berlin Civil Air Transport Advisory Group
BCZ	Berlin Control Zone
BE	British Embassy
BEA	British European Airways
BJSM	British Joint Services Mission, Washington
BK/L	Berlin *Kommandatura*/ Letter
BK/O	Berlin *Kommandatura*/ Order
BM Berlin	British Mission, Berlin
BMG	British Military Government
BOAC	British Overseas Airways Corporation
BRIXMIS	British C-in-C's Mission to the Soviet Forces in Germany

BSSO	British Services Security Organisation	COMECON (CMEA)	Council for Mutual Economic Assistance
BUP	British United Press	COMED	Commercial Management and Exports Department, FCO
CALTF	Combined Air Lift Task Force	COS	Chiefs of Staff
CAS	Chief of the Air Staff	CP	Cabinet Paper
CBS	Columbia Broadcasting System	CPSU	Communist Party of the Soviet Union
CCG BE	Control Commission for Germany (British Element)	CRD	Cultural Relations Department, FCO
CCS	Combined Chiefs of Staff	CRO	Commonwealth Relations Office
CDS	Chief of the Defence Staff	CSBM	Confidence and Security Building Measure
CDU	*Christlich Demokratische Union*/Christian Democratic Union	CSCE	Conference on Security and Cooperation in Europe
CENTO	Central Treaty Organ-sation	CSU	*Christlich-Sozciale Union in Bayern*/Christian Social Union of Bavaria
CFE	Conventional Forces in Europe	DA	Defence Adviser/Attaché
CFM	Council of Foreign Ministers	DAFSD	Director, Air Force Supply Directorate
CIA	Central Intelligence Agency	DBPO	*Documents on British Policy Overseas*
CICC (G)	Commanders-in-Chief Committee (Germany)	DDR	*Deutsche Demokratische Republik*/German Democratic Republic
CIGS	Chief of the Imperial General Staff	DGB	*Deutscher Gewerkschaftsbund*/German Confederation of Trades Unions
C-in-C	Commander-in-Chief	DIW	*Deutsches Institut für Wirstschaftsforschung*/German Institute for Economic Research
COCOM	Coordinating Committee of the Paris Consultative Group	DKP	*Deutsche Kommunistische Partei*/German Communist Party
COI	Central Office of Information	DLT	*Deutsche Luftverkehrgesellschaft*/German Air Traffic Company

DM	Deutsche Mark
DME	East German DM
DMO	Director of Military Operations
DNATO	Director NATO
DO	Dominions Office
DofE	Department of the Environment
DPA	*Deutsche Presse Agentur*/ German Press Agency
DSO	Distinguished Service Order
DTI	Department of Trade and Industry
DTp	Department of Transport
DUS	Deputy Under-Secretary of State
EBF	*Euro-Berlin France*
EC	European Community/ Communities
ECD(E)	European Community Department (External), FCO
ECD(I)	European Community Department (Internal), FCO
EEC	European Economic Community
EED	Eastern European Department, FCO
FCC	Federal Constitutional Court
FCO	Foreign and Common-Wealth Office
FDGB	*Freier Deutscher Gewerkschaftsbund*/Free German Trade Union Federation
FDP	*Freie Demokratische Partei*/ Free Democratic Party
FMOD	Federal Ministry of Defence
FMOF	Federal Ministry of Finance
FO	Foreign Office
FRG	Federal Repulic of Germany
GCA	Ground Control Approach radar system
GDR	German Democratic Republic
GOC	General Officer Commanding
GOC-in-C	General Officer Commanding-in-Chief
GS	General Staff
HC	High Commissioner
HCDC	House of Commons Defence Committee
HMG	Her/His Majesty's Government
HMSO	Her/His Majesty's Stationery Office
HMT	Her/His Majesty's Treasury
IAD	International Aviation Department, DTp
IARA	Inter-Allied Reparations Agency
IASTA	International Air Services Transit Agreement
IATA	International Air Transport Association
ICAO	International Civil Aviation Organisation
ICBM	Inter-continental Ballistic Missile
IDC	Imperial Defence College
IFT	Immediately following telegram
IGB	Inner German Border

IMF	International Monetary Fund
IMG	Information Management Group, FCO
INF/INFO	Information Department, FCO
IPD	Information Policy Department, FO
IRBM	Intermediate Range Ballistic Missile
JAU	Joint Assistance Unit, FCO
JIC	Joint Intelligence Committee
JSM	Joint Services Meeting/Mission
KGB	*Komitet Gosudarstvennoi Besopasnosti*/Committee of State Security
KPD	*Kommunistische Partei Deutschlands*/Communist Party of Germany
LCS	London Controlling Section
LDP	*Liberal-Demokratische Partei*/Liberal Democratic Party
LTC	Long term costing
MAED	Maritime, Aviation and Environment Department, FCO
MAFF	Ministry of Agriculture, Fisheries and Food
MASCO	Middle East Aircraft Servicing Company
MBFR	Mutual and Balanced Force Reductions
MEA	Middle East Airlines
MFA	Ministry of Foreign Affairs
MIFT	My Immediately Following Telegram
MIPT	My Immediately Preceding Telegram
MLM	Military Liaison Mission
MoD/MODUK	Ministry of Defence
MP	Member of Parliament
NAC	North Atlantic Council
NAD	North America Department, FCO
NATO	North Atlantic Treaty Organisation
ND	*Neues Deutschland*
NENAD	Near East and North Africa Department, FCO
NSC	National Security Council
NVA	*Nationale Volksarmee/GDR People's Army*
NWDR	*Nordwestdeutscher Rundfunk*
OCB	Operations Coordinating Board
PDS	*Partei des Demokratischen Sozialismus*/Party of Democratic Socialism
PID	Political Intelligence Department, FO
PM	Prime Minister
POD	Personnel Operations Department
POW	Prisoner of War
PPS	Principal Private Secretary
PQ	Parliamentary Question
PR	Public Relations
PS	Private Secretary

PSD	Personnel Services Department, FCO
PUS	Permanent Under-Secretary of State
PUSD	Permanent Under-Secretary's Department, FCO
QA	Quadripartite Agreement
QRR	Quadripartite Rights and Responsibilities
RAD	Research Analysts Department, FCO
RAF	Royal Air Force
RAF(G)	Royal Air Force (Germany)
RD	Research Department, FO/FCO
RMD	Resource Management Department, FCO
RN	Royal Navy
SACEUR	Supreme Allied Command Europe
SAGW	Surface to Air Guided Weapons
SBU	Strategic Business Unit
SEATO	South East Asia Treaty Organisation
Sec Pol	Security Policy Department, FCO
SED	*Sozialistische Einheitspartei Deutschlands*/Socialist Unity Party of Germany
SEW	*Sozialistische Einheitspartei Westberlins*/Socialist Unity Party of West Berlin
Sigint	Signals intelligence
SISO	Senior Information Services Officer
SMA	*Sowjetische Militäradministration Deutschlands*/Soviet Military Administration of Germany
SOFA	Status of Forces Agreement
SOXMIS	Soviet Military Liaison
SPD	*Sozialdemokratistische Partei Deutschlands*/German Social Democrat Party
SPD	*Sozialdemokratistische Partei Deutschlands*/German Social Democrat Party
SRC	Supreme Restitution Court
SU	Signals Unit
TASS	Telegraph Agency of the Soviet Union
TAUSA	Tempelhof Airlines USA
TTD	Temporary Travel Document
TUR	Telegram Under Reference
TWA	Trans World Airlines
UAR	United Arab Republic
UK	United Kingdom
UKDEL	UK Delegation
UKMIS	UK Mission
UKREP	UK Representative
UN(O)	United Nations (Organisation)
UNGA	UN General Assembly
UNSC	UN Security Council
US(A)	United States (of America)
USAF	US Air Force

USCOS	US Chiefs of Staff
USSR	Union of Soviet Socialist Republics
VOPO	*Volkspolizei*/GDR People's Police
WED	Western European Department, FCO
WGF	West German forces
WOD	Western Organisations Department, FCO
WOPD	Western Organisations Policy Department, FO
WP	*Washington Post*

LIST OF PERSONS

Abbott-Watt, Thorhilda M V, Second Secretary, British Embassy, Bonn, 1988-91

Acheson, Dean G, Under-Secretary of State, US State Department, 1945-49; Secretary of State, 1949-52

Acland, Sir Antony A, APS to the Secretary of State for Foreign Affairs, 1959-62; British Ambassador, Washington, 1986-91

Adam-Schwaetzer, Irmgard, Federal German Minister of State, Ministry of Foreign Affairs, 1987-91

Adams, Geoffrey D, PS to PUS, FCO, 1987-91

Adams, Philip G D, Counsellor, FO, 1959-63

Addison, 1st Viscount (Christopher Addison), Paymaster-General, 1948-49; Lord Privy Seal, 1947-51

Adenauer, Konrad, Chairman, CDU in the British zone of Germany, 1946-48; Federal German Chancellor, 1949-63

Ahrendt, Lothar, GDR Interior Minister, 1989-90

Alexander, Albert V, Minister of Defence, 1947-50

Alexander, Sir Michael O'D B, UK Permanent Representative, NATO, Brussels, 1986-92

Alexandrov, Gen, head of the Soviet air force in Germany, 1948; Soviet representative on the Anglo-Soviet Commission of Inquiry into the Gratow air disaster, 1948

Alphand, Hervé, Director General of Economic, Financial and Technical Affairs, French Foreign Ministry, 1944-49

Amery, Julian, Parliamentary Under-Secretary of State, Colonial Office, 1958-60; Secretary of State of Air, 1960-62

Amrehn, Franz K, *Bürgermeister* (Mayor) of West Berlin, 1955-63; acting *Regierender Bürgermeister* (Governing Mayor) of West Berlin, August-October 1957

Andrusyszyn, Walter E, Special Assistant to the Assistant Secretary for Europe and Canada, US State Department, 1987-88; US Embassy, Bonn, 1988-92

Anne, Princess Royal of Great Britain and Northern Ireland, 1987-

Appleyard, Leonard V, British Ambassador, Budapest, 1986-89; on secondment to the Cabinet Office as Deputy Secretary, 1989-91

Aquino, Maria C C (Cory), President of the Philippines, 1986-92

Arkwright, Paul T, Second Secretary (Chancery) BMG Berlin, 1988-91

Arnold, Karl, Minister-President of North Rhine-Westphalia, 1947-50

Asquith, Herbert H, Prime Minister, 1908-16

Attlee, Clement R, Prime Minister, 1945-51

Austin, John A, Second Secretary, FCO, 1983-2000

Axen, Hermann, member, Politburo of the Central Committee, SED, with responsibilities for international relations, 1970-89

Bache, Andrew P F, Head, PSD, FCO, 1988-90

Bahr, Egon K-H, member of *Bundestag*, 1972-90; SPD inner-German spokesman, 1989

Baker, James A, US Secretary to the Treasury, 1985-88; Secretary of State, 1989-92

Bapst, Gen Charles, French Deputy Commandant, Berlin, 1949

Barclay, Roderick E, Head of Personnel Department, FO, 1946-49; PS to the Secretary of State for Foreign Affairs, 1949-51

Barker, William, Counsellor, British Embassy, Moscow, 1947-51

Barnes, Alfred, Minister of Transport, 1946-51

Barrett, Stephen J, Second Secretary (Deputy Political Adviser), BMG Berlin, 1959-60

Batov, Gen Pavel I, Red Army officer; Commander Baltic Military District, 1958-60; Commander, Soviet Southern Army Group (Hungary), 1960-62

Bayne, Sir Nicholas P, DUS (Economic), FCO, 1988-92

Beam, Jacob D, Chief, Central European Division, US State Department, 1947-49

Beamish, Adrian J, British Ambassador, Lima, 1987-89; AUS (Americas), FCO, 1989-94

Beasley, J A 'Jack', Australian High Commissioner, London, 1946-49

Beauchataud, Francis, Minister-Counsellor (from 1988 Minister Plenitpotentiary), French Embassy, Moscow, 1985-89; Minister assistant to Head of French Military Government and Deputy Commandant, Berlin, 1989-90; Head of the Berlin office of the French Embassy, Bonn, 1990-92

Bebel, August F, leading German socialist, co-founder and chairman of the SPD, 1840-1913

Beetham, Roger C, Head, MAED, FCO, 1985-90

Behrendt, Heinz, head, Office of Inter-German Trade, GDT Ministry of Foreign and Inter-German Trade, 1961

Beil, Gerhard, GDR External Economics Minister, 1986-1990; member, Central Committee, SED, 1981-89

Beith, John G S, Head, Levant Department, FO, 1959-61

Bergmann-Pohl, Sabine, President (Parliamentary Speaker), GDR *Volkskammer*, 1990

Bernadotte, Folke, Count af Wisborg, Swedish diplomat; UN mediator in Palestine, 1948

Bertele, Franz, FRG Permanent Representative in East Berlin 1989-90

Besancenot, Bertrand, Second Counsellor, French Permanent Mission to NATO, Brussels, 1988-90

Bevan, James D, Second, later First, Secretary, UKDEL NATO, Brussels, 1986-90

Bevan, Aneurin, Minister of Health, 1945-51

Bevin, Ernest, Secretary of State for Foreign Affairs, 1945-51

Bidault, Georges-Augustin, French Prime Minister, 1946, 1949-50, 1958

Birch, John Allan, Head, EED, FCO, 1983-86

Birley, Sir Robert, Educational Adviser, British zone of Germany, 1947-49

Bischoff-Pflanz, Heidi, AL (Green) *Fraktion* leader, Berlin House of Representatives, 1989-90

Bishop, Frederick A, Deputy Secretary of the Cabinet, 1959-61

Bishop, Kenneth Anthony, Principal Conference Interpreter, FCO, 1968-98; Research Counsellor, FCO, 1981-98

Bitov, Oleg, special correspondent, *Literaturnaya Gazeta*, 1989

Blake-Pauley, Anthony F, Consul-General, Munich, 1988-92

Blankenhorn, Herbert A von, Federal German Permanent Representative to NATO, 1955-58; Ambassador, Paris, 1958-63

Blatherwick, David E S, AUS (Principal Finance Officer and Chief Inspector), FCO, 1989-91

Bligh, Timothy J, PPS to the Prime Minister, 1959-64

Blot, Jacques, Europe Director, French Foreign Ministry, 1989

Blum, André Léon, French Prime Minister, 1936-37, 1938, 1946-47

Bohlen, Charles E, Special Assistant to the US Secretary of State, 1946-47; Counsellor, US State Department, 1947-49; Minister, US Embassy, Paris, 1949-51; Special Assistant to US Secretary of State, 1959-62

Böhme, Hans-Joachim, member of SED Central Committee, 1973-89; GDR Minister for University and Technical School Affairs, 1970-89

Boidevaix, Serge M-G, French Ambassador, Bonn, 1986-92

Bölke, Joachim, journalist, *Der Tagesspiegel*, Berlin, 1989

Bolz, Lothar, GDR Minister of Foreign Affairs, 1953-1965

Bondarenko, Alexander P, Head of the Third Department, Soviet Foreign Ministry, 1971-91

Boon, G Peter R, News Department, FCO, 1986-90

Bouchez, Aurélia, Central European Department, French Foreign Ministry, 1990

Bourbon-Busset, Jacques de, Deputy Chief, Southern European Division, French Foreign Ministry, 1948

Bourne, Maj-Gen Geoffrey K, British Commandant, Berlin, 1949-51

Bowles, Francis G, Vice-Chairman Parliamentary Labour Party, 1946-48; Deputy Chairman of Ways and Means Committee, 1948-50

Boyd, Sir John D, DUS (Defence), FCO, 1987-89; DUS (Chief Clerk), FCO, 1989-92

Boyd-Carpenter, Maj-Gen The Hon Thomas P J, Chief of Staff, BAOR, 1988-89; Assistant Chief of Defence Staff (Programmes), 1989-92

Bradley, Gen Omar N, US Army Chief of Staff, 1948-49; Permanent Chairman of US Joint Chiefs of Staff, 1949-53

Braithwaite, Sir Rodric, British Ambassador, Moscow, 1988-92

Bramuglia, Dr Juan A, Argentine Foreign Minister, 1946-49

Brandt, Willy, *Regierender Bürgermeister*, West Berlin, 1957-66; Federal German Chancellor, 1969-74

Braun, Carola von, Delegate with responsibility for women, Berlin *Senat*, 1984-90; FDP Land President, Berlin, 1990-94

Braunton, Pat, official, International Aviation Directorate, Department of Transport, 1988

Brentano, Heinrich von, Chairman CDU/CSU Group, *Bundestag*, 1949-55 and 1961-64

Brewer, Nicola M, First Secretary, FCO, PS to Minister of State, 1990-91

Bridges, Sir Edward E, Secretary to the Cabinet, 1938-46; Permanent Secretary to the Treasury, 1946-56

Brimelow, Thomas, Head of Northern Department, FO, 1956-60; Counsellor, Washington, 1960-63

Brook, Sir Norman C, Secretary to the Cabinet, 1947-62

Brooke, Henry, Minister of Housing and Local Government and Minister for Welsh Affairs, 1957-61; Chief Secretary to the Treasury and Paymaster-General, 1961-62

Brooking, Maj-Gen Patrick G, British Commandant, Berlin, 1985-89

Broomfield, Nigel H R A, British Ambassador, East Berlin, 1988-90; DUS (Defence), FCO, 1990-93

Brownjohn, Gen Nevil C D, Chief of Staff and Deputy Military Governor, Control Commission for Germany (British Element), 1947-49

Bullard, Julian L, Second Secretary, Northern Department, FO, 1960-63; British Ambassador, Bonn, 1984-88

Burns, David A, Head of NAD, FCO, 1988-91

Burns, R Andrew, Head of News Department FCO, 1986-90

Burrows, Reginald A, Counsellor and Head of IPD, FO, 1960-61

Burton, Michael St E, Minister and Deputy Commandant, BMG Berlin, 1985-90; Minister and Head of British Embassy Berlin Office, 1990-92

Bush, George H B, US Vice-President, 1981-89; President, 1989-93

Butler, Richard A, Home Secretary, 1957-62

Buwitt, Dankward, Chairman, CDU-*Fraktion*, House of Representatives, Berlin, 1988-91

Buxton Paul W J, Second, then First, Secretary, UKDEL New York, 1956-60; First Secretary, Western Department, FO, 1960-62

Caccia, Sir Harold A, Chief Clerk, FO, 1946-49; British Ambassador, Washington, 1956-61

Cadogan, Sir Alexander, UK Permanent Representative to the UN, New York, 1946-50

Caffery, Jefferson, US Ambassador, Paris, 1944-49

Campbell Alan H, Assistant, News Department, FO, 1958-61; Counsellor and Head of Chancery, UKMIS New York, 1961-65

Cann, Gen François, French Commandant, Berlin, 1987-90

Cannon, Gen John K,Commanding General, US Air Forces in Europe, 1948-51

Carbonnel, Eric C M de, Secretary-General, French Foreign Ministry, 1959-65

Carrick, Roger J, AUS, FCO, 1988-90

Carstens, Karl, Head, European Division, Federal German Foreign Ministry, 1958-60; State-Secretary, 1960-66; Deputy Federal Minister of Foreign Affairs, 1961-66

Carter, Nicholas P, First Secretary, WED, FCO, 1990-94

Carter, Peers L, Counsellor, British Embassy, Washington, 1958-61; Head of UKMIS Geneva, 1961-63

Casey, Richard G, Australian Minister for External Affairs, 1951-60

Cassels, Gen A James H, C-in-C, BAOR, and Commander, NATO Northern Army Group, 1960-63

Ceausescu, Nicolae, General Secretary, Romanian Communist Party, 1965-89; Romanian President, 1967-89

Chalker (Baroness from 1992), Lynda, Minister of State, FCO, 1986-97; Minister for Overseas Development, 1989-97

Chand, Khub, Maj-Gen, Head, Indian Military Mission in Germany, 1948-50

Channon, H Paul G, Secretary of State for Transport, 1987-89

Charles, Sir Noel H H, British Deputy for Italian Colonies on the CFM, 1947-49; British Ambassador, Ankara, 1949-52

Charlton, Alan, First Secretary (Deputy Political Adviser), BMG Berlin, later BM Berlin and British Embassy Office Berlin, 1986-90

Chassard, Dominique, Minister Counsellor, French Embassy, Bonn, 1989-85

Chauvel, Jean, French Foreign Ministry, 1946-49; Ambassador to the UN, New York, 1949-52; Ambassador, London, 1955-62

Cheshire, Group Captain G Leonard, 1917-1992; RAF officer, 1939-45; subsequently peace activist and disabled-rights campaigner

Chevènement, Jean-Pierre, French Defence Minister, 1988-91

Churchill, Winston S, Prime Minister, 1940-45 and 1951-55; leader of HM Opposition, 1945-51

Chuter-Ede, James, Home Secretary, 1945-51

Clark, Gen Mark W, Commander, UN forces in Korea, 1952-53; President, The Citadel, The Military College of South Carolina, Charleston, 1954-66

Clausonne, François S de, French Ambassador, Bonn, 1958-62

Clay, Gen Lucius D, US Military Governor, Germany, and C-in-C, European Command, 1947-49; Personal Representative of the President, with rank of Ambassador, Berlin, 1961-62

Coates, Sir Eric T, Chief of Finance Division, Control Commission Germany (British Element) and Financial Adviser to British High Commissioner, Germany, 1947-49

Cooper, Robert F, Head, Policy Planning Staff, FCO, 1989-93

Corbett, Maj-Gen Robert J S,GOC, Berlin (British Sector) and British Commandant, Berlin, 1989-90; attached to HQ BAOR, 1990-91

Cornwall-Jones, Brig Arthur T, Senior Assistant Secretary (Military) of the Cabinet, 1946-50

Couve de Murville, Maurice, French Foreign Minister, 1958-68

Cox, Nigel J, First Secretary, British Embassy, Paris, 1985-90

Crawford, Robert S, AUS, German Finance Department, FO, 1946-52

Cripps, Sir R Stafford, Chancellor of the Exchequer, 1947-50

Cunningham, Adm Sir John H D, First Sea Lord and Chief of Naval Staff, 1946-48

Dain, David J M, Head, WED, FCO, 1986-90; attached to the Civil Service Commission Recruitment Board, 1989-90

Dalton, E Hugh J N, Chancellor of the Duchy of Lancaster, 1948-50

Dana, Thierry, assistant to the Political Director of the French Foreign Ministry in the two-plus-four negotiations on German unification, 1990

Day, Sir A Cecil, New Zealand Liaison Officer for Foreign Affairs, 1936-52

Dean, Maurice J, DUS, FO (German Section), 1947-48; Deputy Secretary, MoD, 1948-52; PUS, Air Ministry, 1955-63

Dean, (later Sir) Patrick H, Head of German Political Department, FO, 1946-50; DUS, FO, 1956-60; Permanent UK Representative to the UN, New York, 1960-64

Deane, Geoffrey, First Secretary (Chancery), British Embassy, East Berlin, later British Embassy Berlin Office, 1988-91

Deavin, Barbara M, CCG, 1946-47; Hamburg, 1947-50; Berlin, 1950-66; Second (later First) Secretary (*Senat* Liaison Officer), BMG Berlin, 1974-84

Debré, Michel J-P, French Prime Minister, 1959-62

De Freitas, Geoffrey S, Under-Secretary of State for Air, 1946-50

Delacombe, Maj-Gen Rohan, HQ, BAOR, 1949-50; GOC, Berlin (British Sector), 1959-62

Deter, Adolf, Chairman, Berlin FDGB, 1949-51

Dibelius, Otto, Evangelical Bishop of Berlin-Brandenburg, 1945-66

Dickel, Friedrich, GDR Interior Minister, 1963-89

Dickson, Marshal of the RAF Sir William F, Vice Chief of Air Staff, Air Ministry, 1946-48; C-in-C, Middle East Air Force, 1948-50; Chief of Defence Staff, 1958-59

Diepgen, Eberhard, *Regierender Bürgermeister* of West Berlin, 1984-89

Diestel, Peter-Michael, GDR Interior Minister, 1990

Dinwiddy Bruce H, Assistant Secretary, Cabinet Office, 1986-88; Counsellor, British Embassy, Bonn, 1989-1991

Dixon, Sir Pierson J, UK Permanent Representative to the UN, 1954-60; British Ambassador, Paris, 1960-65

Dixon, Robert, Research Department, FCO, 1976-90; RAD, 1990-96

Dobbins, James F, Principal Deputy Assistant Secretary for European and Canadian Affairs, US State Department, 1989-90

Döpfner, Cardinal Julius, Roman Catholic Bishop of Berlin, 1957-61

Dorrer, Wolfgang von, Commissioner for Interzonal and Berlin Transport, Federal German Ministry of Transport, 1959-70

Douglas, Lewis W, US Ambassador, London, 1947-50

Dowling Walter C, US Ambassador, Bonn, 1959-63

Drake, David A, First Secretary (Economic) and Civil Air Attaché, British Embassy, Bonn, 1989-91

Draper, William H, US Under-Secretary of War (later Under-Secretary of Army), 1947-49

Dratvin, Lt-Gen Mikhail I, Deputy C-in-C, Soviet Military Administration for Germany, 1945-49

Drinkall, John K, Western Department, FO, 1957-60

Dudley, Alan A, Counsellor and Head of IPD, FO, 1946-48

Duff, Arthur A, First Secretary, FO, 1957-60; First Secretary, later Counsellor, British Embassy, Bonn, 1960-64

Dufourcq Bertrand, Political Director, French Foreign Ministry, 1988-91

Duggan, Gordon A, Counsellor, COMED, FCO, 1988-89

Duisberg, Claus-Jürgen, Under-Secretary, Federal Chancellery, leader *Arbeitsstab 20*, 1987-90; Federal Interior Ministry, 1990

Dulles, Allen W, Director, CIA, 1953-62

Dulles, John Foster, US Secretary of State, 1953-59

Dumas, Roland, French Foreign Minister, 1988-93

Duncan, Col Andrew, Staff Analyst (later Assistant Director of Information), International Institute for Strategic Studies, London, 1990

Durbrow, Elbridge, Deputy US Representative to the NATO Council of Ministers, Paris, 1961

Eagleburger, Lawrence S, US Deputy Secretary of State, 1989-92

Ebert, Fiedrich ('Fritz') jnr, *Oberbürgermeister* (Lord Mayor), East Berlin, 1948-67

Eccles, Sir David McA, Secretary of State for Education, 1959-62

Eckert, Albert, (AL) Green, Deputy President, Berlin House of Representatives, 1990

Edelsten, Vice-Adm Sir John, Lord Commissioner of the Admiralty and Vice Chief of Naval Staff, 1947-49

Eden, R Anthony, Deputy Leader of the Opposition, 1945-51

Edgar, C George, First Secretary, FCO, 1988-92

Edwards, Ness, Parliamentary Secretary, Ministry of Labour and National Service, 1945-50

Egeland, Leif, South African High Commissioner, London, 1948-50

Eichler, Willy, North Rhine-Westphalia member of the Executive Committee of the SPD, 1948

Eisenhower, Dwight D, Chief of Staff US Army, 1945-48; US President, 1953-61

Eitel, Antonius, Deputy Director-General, Legal Affairs, Federal German Foreign Ministry, 1987-92

Elizabeth, Queen of Great Britain and Ireland, 1936-52; Queen Mother, 1952-2002

Elizabeth II, Queen of Great Britain and Northern Ireland, 1952-

Eppelmann, Rainer, GDR Minister without Portfolio, 1990; Defence Minister, 1990

Erhard, Professor Ludwig, Federal German Minister of Economic Affairs, 1949-63; Vice-Chancellor, 1957-63

Etzdorf, Hasso von, Deputy Under-Secretary of State, Federal German Foreign Ministry, 1958-61; FRG Ambassador, London, 1961-65

Evatt, Herbert V, Australian Attorney-General and Minister for External Affairs, 1941-49; Deputy Prime Minister, 1946-49; President of the UN General Assembly, 1948-49

Everard, Timothy J, British Ambassador, East Berlin, 1984-88

Ewan, Valerie, APS to Minister of State, FCO, 1988-91

Eyers, Patrick H C, British Ambassador, East Berlin, 1990

Fall, Brian J P, AUS (Defence), FCO, 1986-88; Minister, British Embassy, Washington, 1988-89

Fairweather, Patrick S, AUS, FCO, 1987-90

Fearn, P Robin, AUS (Americas), FCO, 1986-89; British Ambassador, Madrid, 1989-94

Fergusson, Sir Ewen A J, British Ambassador, Paris, 1987-92

Festing, Field-Marshal Francis W, Chief of the Imperial General Staff, 1958-61

Fischer, Oskar, SED Central Committee member, 1971-89; GDR Minister for Foreign Affairs, 1975-90

Flower, Robert P, Counsellor, British Embassy, Bonn, 1985-90; Counsellor and Deputy Head of Mission, The Hague, 1990-93

Foggon, George, seconded from RAF Volunteer Reserve to FO, 1946; staff of Military Government, Berlin, 1946-49; Principal, Colonial Office, 1949-51

Ford, Robert A D, First Secretary, Canadian High Commission, London, 1948-51

Foster, Air Vice-Marshal Robert M, Assistant Chief of Air Staff (Policy), 1947-49

Franks, Sir Oliver, British Ambassador, Washington, 1948-53

Freeman, Roger N, Parliamentary Under-Secretary of State for the Armed Forces, 1986-88; Parliamentary Under-Secretary of State, Department of Health, 1988-90; Minister of State, Department of Transport, 1990-94

Freer, Brig Ian L, Chief, BRIXMIS (Berlin), 1989-91

Fretwell, Sir M John E, Political Director and Deputy to the PUS, FCO, 1987-90

Frohnert, Inge, Deputy President, Berlin House of Representatives, 1990

Fulbright, James W, US Senator (Democrat, Arkansas), 1945-74; Chairman, Senate Foreign Relations Committee, 1959-74

Gailey, Brig-Gen Charles K, Chief of Staff, US Office of Military Government, Germany, 1945-48

Gaitskell, Hugh T N, Minister of Fuel and Power, 1947-50

Garran, I Peter, seconded to Control Commission, Germany, Chief of Political Division, Berlin, 1947-50

Gallacher, William, Communist MP, Western Division of Fife, 1935-50

Galleghan, Maj-Gen Frederick G, Head, Australian Military Mission in Germany, 1948-49

Garel-Jones, W A T Tristan, Minister of State, FCO, 1990-93

Gaulle, Gen Charles A J M de, French Prime Minister, 1958-59; President, 1959-69

Gayk, Andreas, *Oberbürgermeister*, Kiel, 1946-54

Genscher, Hans-Dietrich, Federal German Foreign Minister and Deputy Chancellor, 1974-92

Geraghty, William, Assistant Under-Secretary, War Office, 1958-60; Under-Secretary, Cabinet Office, 1960-62

Gerlach, Manfred, GDR Chairman of the Council of State (Head of State), 1989-90

Gerstenmaier, Eugen K A, Acting CDU Federal Chairman, 1956-66; *Bundestag* President, 1954-69

Gilchrist, Andrew G, FO, 1946-51

Gillmore, Sir David H, DUS (Americas/Asia), FCO, 1986-89

Gifford, C H P, Assistant Secretary, Economic Department, FO German Section, 1947-48; Deputy Financial Adviser, Berlin Office of the Financial Adviser, 1948-49

Given, Edward F, FO, 1946-49; Second Secretary, Paris, 1949-51

Glenarthur, Lord, Minister of State, FCO, 1987-89

Glover, Audrey F, First Secretary (Legal Adviser), BMG Berlin, 1985-89; Legal Counsellor, FCO, and UK Agent to European Commission and Court of Human Rights, 1990-94

Glover, Edward C, Senate Liaison Officer, BMG Berlin, 1985-89; Deputy Head, NENAD, FCO, 1989-91

Gniffke, Erich W, member, SED Central Executive, Berlin, and Chairman of the People's Council, 1945-48

Goldsmith, Alexander K, British Consul-General, Hamburg, 1986-90

Goodman, Andrew L, East-West Coordinator, European Bureau, US State Deptartment, 1990

Gorbachev, Mikhail S, General Secretary of the Central Committee of the CPSU, 1985-91; Soviet President, 1988-91

Gordon, C A, PS to Minister of State for the Armed Forces, 1987-88

Gordon-Walker, Patrick C, Parliamentary Under-Secretary of State, CRO, 1947-50

Gore-Booth, Hon David A, Head, Policy Planning Staff, FCO, 1987-89; AUS (Middle East), FCO, 1989-93

Gore-Booth, Sir Paul, DUS, FO, 1957-61

Goulden, P John, Head of Chancery, UKREP Brussels, 1984-88; AUS (Defence), FCO, 1988-92

Gozney, Richard H T, APS (later PPS) to the Secretary of State for Foreign and Commonwealth Affairs, 1989-93

Grainger, John A, Assistant Legal Adviser, FCO, 1984-89; First Secretary (Legal Adviser) BMG (later BM) Berlin, 1989-91

Greenstock, Jeremy Q, Head of Chancery, British Embassy, Paris, 1987-90; AUS, FCO, 1990-93

Grey, Sir Edward, Foreign Secretary, 1905-16

Griffiths, Howard, AUS (Policy), MoD, 1988-91

Grinin, Vladimir M, Political Counsellor Soviet Embassy East Berlin, 1989

Gromyko, Andrei A, Soviet Representative, UNSC, 1946-48; Soviet Deputy Foreign Minister, 1946-49; Foreign Minister, 1957-85

Gronchi, Giovanni, Italian President, 1955-62

Grotewohl, Otto, Member, SED Politburo, 1946-64; SED Co-Chairman, 1946-50; GDR Prime Minister, 1949-64

Gueffroy, Chris, East Berliner, the last man to die trying to cross the Berlin Wall, 1989

Guelluy, Philippe G, Head of the Disarmament and Strategic Affairs Section, French Foreign Ministry, 1988-92

Gummer, John S, Minister of State, MAFF, 1985-88; Minister of State, DoE, 1988-89; Minister of Agriculture, Fisheries and Food, 1989-93

Gysi, Gregor, Chairman, SED, PDS, 1990-98

Haddock, Maj-Gen Raymond E, US Commandant, Berlin, 1988-90

Haffner, Sebastian (born Raimund Pretzel), German journalist and writer; German correspondent of *The Observer* in Berlin, 1954-61

Hailsham, Viscount, Quintin McG Hogg, Deputy Leader, House of Lords, 1957-60; Lord President of the Council, 1957-59 and 1960-64; Lord Privy Seal, 1959-60; Minister for Science and Technology, 1959-64; Leader of the House of Lords, 1960-63

Hall, Viscount (George Henry Hall), First Lord of the Admiralty, 1946-51; Deputy Leader of the House of Lords, 1947-51

Hallstein, Walter, President, EEC Commission, Brussels, 1958-67

Hancock, Patrick F, Head, Western Department, FO, 1956-59

Hankey, Hon Robert M A, Head, Northern Department, FO, 1946-49

Harding, Air Vice-Marshal Peter J, Deputy C-in-C, RAF, Germany, 1989-91

Harding, Marshal Sir Peter R, Air Officer Commanding-in-Chief, RAF Strike Command and C-in-C, UK Air Forces, 1985-88; Chief of Air Staff, 1988-92

Hare, John H, Minister of Agriculture, Fisheries and Food, 1958-60; Minister of Labour, 1960-63

Harriman, W Averill, US Secretary of Commerce, 1946-48; US Special Representative in Europe under Economic Cooperation Act of 1948, 1948-50; US Representative on North Atlantic Defence, Financial and Economic Committee, 1949; US Ambassador-at-Large, 1961

Harrison, Geoffrey W, Minister, British Embassy, Moscow, 1947-49

Hartland-Swann, Julian D N, British Consul-General, Frankfurt-am-Main, 1986-90

Harvey, Sir Oliver C, British Ambassador, Paris, 1948-54

Hawtin, Brian R, PS to Secretary of State for Defence, 1987-89; AUS (material/naval), MoD, 1989-92

Hartmann, Peter, Head of Group 21, Federal German Chancellery, 1987-91

Hays, Maj-Gen George P, Commanding General, Office of the US Military Government in Germany; Deputy US Military Governor for Germany, 1947-49

Hayter, William G, AUS, FO, 1948-49; Minister, British Embassy, Paris, 1949-53

Hedley, E W L, Head of Secretariat Policy (NATO/UK), MoD, 1989-91

Heine, Fritz, member, SPD Executive Committee, 1946-59

Hemans, Simon N P, Head, Soviet Department, FCO, 1987-90

Henderson, Arthur, Secretary of State for Air, 1947-51

Henderson, Lord, Economic Secretary to the Treasury, 1945-50

Henderson, John N, Assistant, Soviet Section, Northern Department, FO, 1959-63

Henneberg, Willy, President, Berlin House of Representatives, 1958-61

Herold, Eckart, Federal German Foreign Ministry, Bonn, 1988-91

Herter, Christian A, US Under-Secretary of State, 1957-59; Secretary of State, 1959-61

Hertz, Dr Paul, SPD Senator for Economic and Financial Affairs, Berlin House of Representatives, 1955-61

Herwarth von Bittenfeld, Hans H, Federal German Ambassador, London, 1955-61; State-Secretary and Chief of the Federal Presidential Office, 1961-65

Hess, W R Rudolf, German Deputy *Führer*, 1933-41; prisoner, Spandau prison, Berlin, 1946-87

Heydon, Peter R, Counsellor, Australian High Commission, London, 1947-50

Heym, Stefan (born Helmut Flieg), 1913-2001; German-Jewish writer, resident in GDR from 1953

Hill, Charles, Chancellor of the Duchy of Lancaster, 1957-61; Minister of Housing and Local Government and Minister for Welsh Affairs, 1961-62

Hill, P Jeremy O, First Secretary (Legal Adviser), British Embassy, Bonn, 1987-90

Hillenbrand, Martin J, Director, Office of German Affairs, US State Department, 1958-62

Hitler, Adolf, German *Führer* and Chancellor, 1933-45

Höynck, Wilhelm, Director for Economic Relations, Director, Eastern Europe, and Alternate Political Director, German Foreign Ministry, 1986-91

Hollis, Lt-Gen Sir Leslie C, Chief Staff Officer to Minister of Defence 1947-49; Deputy Secretary (Military) of the Cabinet, 1947-49; Commandant General, Royal Marines, 1949-52

Holmes, Henry A, Assistant Secretary, Bureau of Political Military Affairs, Washington, 1984-89; US Ambassador-at-Large for Burdensharing, 1989-93

Holmes, John E, First Secretary, British Embassy, Paris, 1984-87; Assistant Head, Soviet Department, FCO, 1988-89

Holmes, Julius C, Minister, US Embassy, London, 1948-53

Home, 14th Earl of, Secretary of State for Foreign Affairs, 1960-63

Honecker, Erich, Full Member of SED Politburo, 1958-90; General Secretary of the SED, 1971-89; GDR Chairman of the Council of State, 1976-89

Honecker, Margot, GDR Minister of National Education, 1963-89

Hood, Viscount Samuel, Minister, British Embassy, Washington, 1957-62

Hooper, Robin W J, Head of PUSD, FO, 1957-60; Assistant Secretary-General (Political Affairs), NATO, 1960-66

Hopper, Paul, General Manager for Germany, BA, 1989

Howe, Sir Geoffrey, Secretary of State for Foreign and Commonwealth Affairs, 1983-89; Lord President of the Council, Leader of the House of Commons and Deputy Prime Minister, 1989-90

Howley, Gen Frank L, US Commandant, Berlin, 1945-49

Hudson, P J, Assistant Principal, Air Ministry, 1948-49

Hulse, Christopher, Head of Eastern European, subsequently Central European, Department, FCO, 1988-92

Hunter, Alistair J, Consul-General, Düsseldorf, and Director-General of Trade and Investment, FRG, 1988-91

Hurd, Douglas R, UKDEL New York, 1956-60; PS to PUS, FO, 1960-63; Home Secretary, 1985-89; Secretary of State for Foreign and Commonwealth Affairs, 1989-95

Inge, Gen Sir Peter A, Commander 1st (British) Corps, 1987-89; Commander, Northern Army Group and C-in-C, BAOR, 1990

Issacs, George A, Minister of Labour and National Service, 1945-51

Jackling, Roger W, AUS, FO, 1959-63

Jay, Michael H, Counsellor (Financial and Commercial), British Embassy, Paris, 1987-90; AUS (EC Affairs), FCO, 1990-93

Jebb, Hubert M Gladwyn (later Lord Gladwyn), AUS, FO, and UN Adviser, 1946-47; UK Representative, Brussels Treaty Permanent Commission, 1948; DUS, FO, 1949-50; British Ambassador, Paris, 1954-60

Jendretzky, Hans, Chairman, Free German Trade Union Federation, 1946-48; member of the Executive Committee of the SED; First Secretary of the SED, 1948-53

Jessup, Philip C, US international lawyer; US representative at various sessions of UN Security Council and General Assembly, 1948-53; Ambassador-at-Large, 1949-53

Johnson, Carol, Secretary of the Parliamentary Labour Party, 1943-59

Johnson, Lyndon B, US Senator (Democrat, Texas), 1949-61; Vice-President, 1961-63

Johnston, Alexander, Under-Secretary, Office of the Lord President of the Council, 1946-48; Deputy Secretary of the Cabinet, 1948-51

Jones, A Creech, Secretary of State for the Colonies, 1946-50

Jones, Sir Cyril E, AUS, FO (German Section), 1947-50

Jones Parry, Emyr, Deputy Head, Office of President of European Parliament, 1987-89; Head, ECD (E), FCO, 1989-93

Jowitt, Viscount, Lord Chancellor, 1945-51

Kaifu, Toshika, Japanese Prime Minister, 1989-91

Kaiser, Jacob, Chairman of the CDU in the Soviet zone of Germany, 1948

Kaldor, Nicholas, Director, Research and Planning Division, Economic Commission for Europe, Geneva, 1947-49

Kastrup, Dieter, Political Director, Federal German Foreign Ministry, 1988-91

Keightley, Gen Sir Charles F, Director of Military Training, War Office, 1946-47; Military Secretary to the Secretary of State for War, 1948; C-in-C, BAOR, 1948-51

Kennan, George F, Director, Policy Planning Staff, US State Department, 1947-49

Kennedy, John F, US Senator (Democrat, Massachusetts), 1953-60; President, 1961-63

Kerr, John O, AUS (European Community), FCO, 1987-90

Khrushchev, Nikita S, First Secretary of Central Committee of the CPSU, 1953-64; Chairman of the Council of Ministers of the USSR, 1958-64

Killick, John E, Assistant Head, Western Department, FO, 1958-62

Kilmuir, Lord (David P Maxwell Fyfe), Lord Chancellor, 1954-62

King, Lord, Chairman, BA, 1981-93

King, Tom (Thomas) J, Secretary of State for Northern Ireland, 1985-89; Secretary of State for Defence, 1989-92

Kinnear, A, Head, German Supply Department, FO, 1948-50

Kirkpatrick, Sir Ivone, DUS, FO, 1948-49; PUS, FO (German Section), 1949-50

Kissinger, Henry A, Associate Professor of Government, Harvard University, 1958-62

Klatt, W, Food and Agriculture Analysis Section, German Supply Department, FO, 1948-49

Klein, Walter, Berlin *Senat* Director, Protocol and Foreign Affairs Office, 1953-63

Klemann, Jürgen, *Bürgermeister*, Berlin-Zehlendorf, 1985-91

Kochemasov, Vladislav I, Soviet Ambassador, East Berlin, 1983-90

Koenig, Gen Marie-Pierre, French C-in-C, Germany, 1945-49

Kohl, Helmut, Federal German Chancellor, 1982-98

Kohler, Foy D, US Deputy Assistant Secretary of State, 1958-59; Assistant Secretary of State (European Affairs), 1959-62

Konev, Marshal Ivan S, Commander, Soviet ground forces and First Deputy Minister of Defence of the Soviet Union, 1946-50; C-in-C, Warsaw Pact Armed Forces, 1956-60; Commander, Soviet forces in the GDR, 1961-62

Kosygin, Alexei N, Deputy Chairman, Council of Ministers of the USSR, 1946-53; Soviet Minister of Finance, 1948; Chairman, State Planning Committee, 1959-60; First Deputy Chairman, Council of Ministers, 1960-64; alternate member, Presidium of CPSU Central Committee, 1957-60; member, Presidium CPSU Central Committee, 1960-66

Kotikov, Gen Aleksandr G, Soviet Commandant, Berlin, 1946-50

Kovalev, Anatolii G, Soviet First Deputy Minister of Foreign Affairs, 1986-92

Krack, Erhard, *Oberbürgermeister*, East Berlin, 1974-90

Kramer, Erwin, GDR Minister of Transport, 1954-70

Krenz, Egon, member, SED Central Committee, 1973-90; Secretary, Central Committee, 1989-90; Politburo member, 1983-90; Politburo Secretary, 1989-90; Deputy Chairman, GDR Council of State, 1984-89; Chairman, Council of State, 1989-90

Kressmann, Willy K E, *Bürgermeister*, Berlin-Kreuzberg, 1949-62

Krishna Menon, V P, Indian High Commissioner, London, 1947-52; Indian Minister of Defence, 1957-62

Kroll, Hans A, Federal German Ambassador, Moscow, 1958-62

Krone, Heinrich, Chairman, CDU Parliamentary Party in the *Bundestag*, 1955-61; Federal German Minister for Special Tasks, 1961-64

Kuhn-Delforge, Jean-Loup, Head, Political Division, French Military Government, Berlin, 1987-89

Künast, Renate, AL (Green), member, Berlin House of Representatives, 1989-2000; speaker, AL *Fraktion*, 1990-93

Kvitsinski, Yuli A, Soviet Ambassador, Bonn, 1986-90; First Deputy to Soviet Foreign Minister, 1990-91

Kyaw, Dietrich von, Head, European Communities Sub-Section, and Deputy Head, Economic Section, Federal German Foreign Ministry, 1989-93

Lacomme, Gen Jean, French Commandant Berlin, 1958-62

Laloy, Jean, Director, European Affairs, French Foreign Ministry, 1956-61

Lamont, Donald A, Counsellor on secondment to International Institute for Labour Studies (IISS), 1988; Counsellor and Head of Chancery, BMG (later BM) Berlin, 1988-91

Lance Andrew R, First Secretary, FCO, 1981-90; transferred to East European Section, RAD, FCO, 1990

Landowsky, Klaus-Rüdiger, General Secretary, Berlin CDU, 1985-91; Deputy Chairman, CDU *Fraktion*, Berlin *Senat*, 1975-90

Langenhove, Fernand van, Belgian Permanent Representative to the UN, 1946-57

Lansdowne, Lord, Joint Parliamentary Under-Secretary of State, FO, 1958-62

Lautenschlager, Hans W, State-Secretary, Federal German Foreign Ministry, 1987-93

Ledwidge, W Bernard J, Political Adviser (Counsellor), British Political Branch, Berlin, 1956-61

Lemmer, Ernst, Federal German Minister for All-German Affairs, 1957-62

Lemnitzer, Gen Lyman L, Vice-Chief of Staff, US Army, 1957-59; Chief of Staff, 1959-60; Chairman Joint Chiefs of Staff, 1960-62

Lenin, Vladimir Ilyich Ulyanov, Chairman of the Council of People's Commissars, Soviet Russia, 1917-24

Leopold, Kurt, Head, FRG Foreign Trade Department, 1947-49; Head of the Berlin bureau of the Trust Office for Interzonal Trade, 1953-65

Lever, Paul J, Head, Security Policy Department, FCO, 1987-90

Lie, Trygve H, UN Secretary-General, 1946-52

Ligachev, Yegor K, member, Central Committee, CPSU, 1976-90; member Politburo, 1985-90; Secretary-Central, Committee in Charge of Personnel and Ideology, 1984-88; Head of Commission on Agriculture, 1988-90

Lightner, Edwyn A, Jr, Minister, US Mission, Berlin, 1959-63

Lilley, Peter B, Economic Secretary to the Treasury, 1987-89; Financial Secretary to the Treasury, 1989-90; Secretary of State for Trade and Industry, 1990-92

Ling, Jeffrey, Director of Resources, FCO, 1986-89; AUS and Director of Communications, subsequently of Information Systems, 1989-96

Linh Nguyen Van, General Secretary, Communist Party of Vietnam, 1986-91

Llewellyn-Smith, Michael C, Head, Soviet Department, FCO, 1985-87; Minister, British Embassy, Paris, 1988-91

Lloyd, J Selwyn B, Secretary of State for Foreign Affairs, 1955-60; Chancellor of the Exchequer, 1960-62

Logan, David B C, Minister and Deputy Head of Mission, British Embassy, Moscow, 1989-92

Lovett, Robert A, US Under Secretary of State, 1947-49

Luke, Stephen E V, Under-Secretary, Cabinet Office, 1947-50

Lukyanchenko, Lt-Gen G S, Chief of Staff, Soviet Military Administration, Germany, 1948

Lunghi, Hugh, British interpreter, 1948

Lyne, Roderic M J, Counsellor and Head of Chancery, British Embassy, Moscow, 1987-90; Head, Soviet Department, FCO, 1990-92

MacDermot, Dermot F, AUS, FO, 1959-61

McDermott, Edward A, Deputy Director, US Office of Civil and Defense Mobilisation, the White House, 1960-61

McDermott, Patrick A, Consul-General and Economic and Financial Adviser, BMG Berlin, 1984-88; First Secretary, FCO, 1988-89; Counsellor, British Embassy, Paris, 1990-95

Machtig, Sir Eric G, PUS, Commonwealth Relations Office, 1940-49

MacLaren of MacLaren, Donald, the, First Secretary, Policy Planning Staff, FCO, 1987-91

McLean, Maj-Gen Kenneth G, Vice-Adjutant-General, War Office, 1947-49; Chief of Staff, Control Commission Germany and Deputy Military Governor, British zone, Germany, 1949; Military Secretary to the Secretary of State for War, 1949-51

Macleod, Iain N, Minister of Labour (and National Service), 1955-59; Secretary of State for the Colonies, 1959-61; Chancellor of the Duchy of Lancaster and Leader of the House of Commons, 1961-63

Macmillan, M Harold, Conservative MP for Bromley, 1945-1964; Prime Minister, 1957-63

McNamara, Robert S, US Secretary of Defense, 1961-68

McNaughton, Gen Hon Andrew G L, Canadian representative, UN Atomic Energy Commission, 1946-49; Permanent Representative, UN, 1948-49

McNeil, Hector, Minster of State, FO, 1946-50

Maizière, Lothar de, GDR Prime Minister, 1990; Federal German Minister for Special Affairs, 1990

Major, John, Chief Secretary, Treasury, 1987-89; Secretary of State for Foreign and Commonwealth Affairs, 1989; Chancellor of the Exchequer, 1989-90; Prime Minister, 1990-97

Makins, Roger M, AUS, FO, 1947-48; DUS, FO, 1948-52

Maleuda, Günther, President (Parliamentary Speaker), GDR *Volkskammer*, 1989-90

Malik, Yakov A, Soviet Deputy Minister of Foreign Affairs, 1946-53; representative to the UN, 1949-52; Ambassador, London, 1953-60; Deputy Foreign Minister, 1960-67

Mallaby, Sir Christopher L G, on secondment to Cabinet Office as a Deputy Secretary, 1985-88; British Ambassador, Bonn, 1988-92

Marett, Robert H K, AUS, FO, 1958-63

Marjoribanks, James A M, Minister (Economic) British Embassy, Bonn, 1957-62

Maron, Karl, GDR Interior Minister, 1955-63

Marples, A Ernest, Postmaster-General, 1957-59; Minister of Transport, 1959-64

Marshall, Gen George C, US Secretary of State, 1947-49

Marshall, Noël H, Minister, British Embassy, Moscow, 1986-89; UK Permanent Representative to the Council of Europe, 1990-93

Marten, Francis W (Tim), First Secretary, British Embassy, Bonn, 1958-60; Counsellor, British Embassy, Bonn, 1960-62

Mason, Sir Paul, British Ambassador, The Hague, 1954-60; UK Permanent Representative to NATO, Paris, 1960-63

Massigli, René, French Ambassador, London, 1944-55

Mates, Lt-Col Michael J, Chairman, House of Commons Select Committee on Defence, 1987-92

Matlock, Jack F, US Ambassador, Moscow, 1987-91

Maude, Francis A A, Parliamentary Under-Secretary of State, DTI, 1987-89; Minister of State, FCO, 1989-90; Financial Secretary to HM Treasury, 1990-92

Maximychev, Igor, Soviet Minister, East Berlin, 1988-90

Mayhew, Christopher P, Parliamentary Under-Secretary of State for Foreign Affairs, 1946-50

Meckel, Markus, GDR Minister of Foreign Affairs, 1990

Meisner, Norbert, Berlin Finance Senator, 1989-90

Mende, Erich, Chairman, FDP *Fraktion, Bundestag,* 1957-63; FDP Chairman, 1960-68

Menzies, Sir Robert G, Australian Prime Minister, 1949-66; Minister for External Affairs, 1960-61

Merchant, Livingston T, US Under-Secretary of State (Political Affairs), 1959-61

Merer, Air Commodore John W F, Director, Allied Cooperation and Foreign Liaison, Air Ministry, 1945-47; Air Officer Commander, No. 46 Group 1947-49; Commander, British element of Berlin Airlift, 1948-49

Merillon, Jean-Marie, French Ambassador, Moscow, 1989-91

Merry, David B, Head of Chancery, British Embassy, East Berlin, 1985-88; First Secretary, FCO, 1989-93

Meyer, Paul, Political Counsellor, Canadian Delegation, NATO, Brussels, 1988-92

Mielke, Erich, GDR Minister of State Security, 1957-89

Mikoyan, Anastas I, First Vice-Chairman, Soviet Council of Ministers, 1955-64

Millar, Sir Frederick R Hoyer, AUS, FO, 1947-48; Minister, British Embassy, Washington, 1948-50; PUS, FO, 1957-62

Mills, Lord, Minister of Power, 1957-59; Paymaster-General, 1959-61; Minister without Portfolio, 1961-62

Mischnick, Wolfgang, Deputy Chairman, FDP, 1964-88

Mittag, Günter, SED Politburo member, 1966-89; Secretary for Economics, SED Central Committee, 1976-89

Mitterand, François M A M, French President, 1981-95

Mitzscherling, Peter, Senator for Economics, Berlin, 1989-90

Modrow, Hans, SED Central Committee member and First Secretary Dresden regional leadership, 1973-89; Chairman of the Council of Ministers of the GDR, 1989-90

Molotov, Vyacheslav M, Soviet Foreign Minister, 1939-49

Momper, Walter, SPD Party Whip, Berlin, 1985-89; *Regierender Bürgermeister*, West Berlin, 1989-91

Montgomery of Alamein, Field-Marshal Viscount Bernard L, CIGS, 1946-48; Chairman of Western Europe Commanders in Chief's Committee, 1948-51

Morrison, Herbert, Deputy Prime Minister, 1945-51; Lord President of the Council and Leader of the House of Commons, 1945-51

Morton, Ralph C, Third, later Second, Secretary (Chancery), British Embassy, East Berlin (later British Embassy, Berlin Office), 1987-91

Moss, David C, Under-Secretary, International Aviation Department, Department of Transport, 1988-93

Mottram, Richard C, AUS, MoD, 1986-89; DUS (Policy), MoD, 1989-92

Murray Francis R H, AUS, FO, 1957-61; DUS, FO, 1961-62

Murray, James, First Secretary, British Embassy Paris, 1957-61; Consul, Usumbura, 1961-62

Murray, Peter, Counsellor, UKDEL NATO, Paris, 1959-61 (Acting UK Representative, 1960)

Munro, Colin A, Counsellor, British Embassy, East Berlin, 1987-90; British Consul-General, Frankfurt-am-Main, 1990-93

Murphy, Robert D, US Political Adviser for Germany; US Deputy for Germany, Council of Foreign Ministers, 1945-49; US Ambassador, Brussels, 1949-52; Deputy Under-Secretary of State, 1954-59; Under-Secretary of State (Political Affairs), 1959

Murrie, William S, Deputy Secretary (Civil), Cabinet Office, 1947; Deputy Under-Secretary of State, Home Office, 1947-52

Myrdal, Prof Karl Gunnar, Swedish Minister of Commerce, 1945-47; Executive Secretary, UN Economic Commission for Europe, Geneva, 1947-57

Nasser, Gamal Abdel, Egyptian President, 1956-70

Naumann, Maj-Gen Klaus, Head of Defence Policy and Operations Staff, FRG Ministry of Defence, 1988-90; Adviser in two-plus-four negotiations on German Unification, 1990

Nazarov, Lt-Col Konstantin, Soviet Military Administration for Germany, 1948

Nehru, Jawaharlal, Indian Prime Minister, 1947-64

Nenni, Pietro, Italian Minister of Foreign Affairs, 1946-47

Neuling, Christian, CDU *Bundestag* representative for Berlin, 1987-94

Neumann, Franz, Berlin member of the SPD Executive Committee, 1948

Neville-Jones, L Pauline, Minister, British Embassy, Bonn, 1987-91

Nichols, Sir Philip B B, British Ambassador, Prague, 1945-48; British Ambassador, The Hague, 1948-52

Nicolson, Sir Harold, 1886-1968, British diplomat (FO, 1909-29), author and politician

Nier, Kurt, GDR Deputy Foreign Minister, 1973-89

Nixon, Richard M, US Vice-President, 1953-61

Noel-Baker, Philip J, Secretary of State for Air, 1946-47; Secretary of State for Commonwealth Relations, 1947-50

Noiret, Gen Roger J C, French Deputy Military Governor for Germany, 1946-51

Norstad, Gen Lauris, C-in-C, US European Command, 1956-62; Supreme Allied Commander, Europe, 1956-62

Northe, Heinrich, Deputy Head, Eastern Department, Federal German Foreign Ministry, 1958-61

Notev, Martin, GDR citizen, who attempted to flee from East to West Berlin, 14 February 1989

Oakeshott, Keith R, First Secretary, British Embassy, Moscow, 1959-61; First Secretary, later Counsellor, British Embassy, Havana, 1961-62

Oliver, Col Richard A, British Commander, Berlin Infantry Brigade, 1988-90

Ollenhauer, Erich, Chairman, SDP, 1952-63

O'Neill, Con D W (from 1962 Sir), FO, 1947-48; seconded to Political Division, Control Commission in Germany, 1948-53; AUS, FO, 1957-60; British Ambassador, Helsinki, 1961-63

O'Neill, Robert J, British Ambassador, Vienna and concurrently Head of the UK Delegation to the MBFR talks, 1986-89; British Ambassador, Brussels, 1989-92

Ormsby-Gore, W David, Minister of State for Foreign Affairs, 1957-61; British Ambassador, Washington, 1961-65

Osborne, Gen Ralph M, US Commandant, Berlin, 1959-61

Pagniez, Yves, French Ambassador, Moscow, 1986-89

Pahlavi, Mohammad Reza, Shah of Iran, 1941-79

Palin, Air Marshal Sir Roger H, C-in-C, RAF, Germany, and Commander, Second Allied Tactical Air Force, 1989-91

Paris, Jacques-Camille, Minister-Counsellor, French Embassy, London, 1945-49

Parker, Sir Harold, Secretary, Ministry of Pensions, 1946-48; Permanent Secretary, Ministry of Defence, 1948-56

Parker, Lyn, First Secretary, FCO, 1984-89 (APS to Secretary of State, 1987-89); Counsellor seconded to the Cabinet Office, 1989-91

Parodi, Alexandre, French Permanent Representative to the UN, 1946-49

Peck, Edward H (from 1966 Sir), Counsellor, British High Commission, Singapore, 1958-61; AUS, FO, 1961-66

Peck, John H, First Secretary, British Embassy, The Hague, 1947-50; UK Permanent Representative to the Council of Europe and Consul-General, Strasbourg, 1959-62

Pestell, Catherine E, AUS (Public Departments), FCO, 1987-89

Peterson, Sir Maurice D, British Ambassador, Moscow, 1946-49

Pfarr, Heidi M, Berlin Senator, responsible for federal affairs, 1989-90

Pfeiffer, Anton, Leader of the CDU/CSU *Fraktion* in the Bavarian parliamentary *Rathaus*, 1948-49

Philip, Prince, Duke of Edinburgh, consort of Queen Elizabeth II, 1952-

Pieck, F Wilhelm R, GDR State President and Chairman, Council of State, 1949-60

Playfair, Edward W, Assistant Secretary, Treasury, 1944-47; Under-Secretary, Treasury, 1947-49; seconded to the Control Commission for Germany and Austria, 1946-47

Pocock, Andrew J, First Secretary, Southern Africa Department, FCO, 1986-87; First Secretary, British Embassy, Washington, 1988-92

Pöhlmann, Jürgen, FRG Representative, NATO, 1989

Poole, Maj-Gen William H E, Deputy Chief, General Staff, Union of South African Defence Force, 1946-48; Head, South African Military Mission in Germany, 1948-51

Pope, Andrew L, First Secretary, later Counsellor, British Embassy, Bonn, 1960-72

Powell, Charles D, PS to the Prime Minister, 1983-91

Powell, Jonathan N, Assistant Head, Policy Planning Staff, FCO, 1989-91

Probst, Albert, Parliamentary State-Secretary, German Federal Ministry for Research and Technology, 1982-91

Profumo, John D, Parliamentary Under-Secretary of State, FO, 1958-59; Minister of State for Foreign Affairs, 1959-60; Secretary of State for War, 1960-63

Qasim, Abd al-Karim, Iraqi Prime Minister, 1958-61

Quayle, J Danforth, US Vice-President, 1989-93

Rakowski, Mieczyslaw F, First Secretary, Polish United Workers' Party Central Committee, 1989-90; Chairman, Council of Ministers, 1988-89

Ralph, Richard P, Counsellor, POD, FCO, 1985-89; Head of Chancery and Congressional Counsellor, British Embassy, Washington, 1989-93

Ramsden, Sir John C J, First Secretary, WED, FCO, 1988-90; Counsellor and Deputy Head of Mission, British Embassy, East Berlin (later British Embassy, Berlin Office), 1990-93

Ramsbotham, Hon Peter E, Assistant (Planning and Coordination), PUSD, 1957-61; Head, Western Organisations and Planning Department, FO, 1961-62

Rapacki, Adam, Polish Foreign Minister, 1956-68

Ratford, David J E, AUS (Europe), FCO, 1986-90

Reagan, Ronald W, US President, 1981-89

Redmayne, Martin, Parliamentary Secretary to the Treasury and Government Chief Whip, 1959-64.

Reich, Prof Jens, leader of *Neues Forum*, GDR, 1989

Reid, Gordon B, First Secretary, WED, 1985-88

Reilly, Sir Patrick, British Ambassador, Moscow, 1957-60; DUS, FO, 1960-64

Rettel, Klaus, CDU Research Associate and *Fraktion* Manager, Berlin House of Representatives, 1970-94

Reuter, Professor Ernst, SPD member, Berlin *Magistrat*; elected, but not confirmed, *Oberbürgermeister*, Berlin, 1947; *Regierender Bürgermeister*, West Berlin, 1948-53

Reuter, Edzard, Chairman of Daimler-Benz, 1987-95

Ribbentrop, Joachim von, German Foreign Minister, 1938-45

Rice, Condoleezza, Special Assistant to the US President for National Security Affairs, NSC, 1989-91; Director to Senior Director, Soviet and East European Affairs, 1989-91; member, US Delegation, two-plus-four talks on German unification

Richthofen, Baron Hermann von, Federal German Ambassador, London, 1989-93

Ricketts, Peter F, First Secretary (Chancery), British Embassy, Washington, 1986-89; First Secretary, later Counsellor, FCO, 1989-94

Riedl, Erich, Parliamentary State-Secretary, Federal German Economics Ministry, 1987-93

Ritchie, Albert E, First Secretary, Canadian High Commission, London, 1948-51

Roberts, Sir Frank, British Minister, Moscow, 1945-47; PPS to the Secretary of State for Foreign Affairs, 1947-49; UK Permanent Representative to NATO, 1957-60; British Ambassador, Moscow, 1960-63

Robertson, Lt-Gen Sir Brian, Deputy C-in-C, British Forces of Occupation, Germany; Deputy British Military Governor for Germany, 1945-47; C-in-C and Military Governor, 1947-49

Robertson, Norman A, Canadian High Commissioner, London, 1946-49

Rodemark, Janet M, WED, FCO, 1988-92

Romberg, Walter, GDR Finance Minister, 1990

Rome, Maj-Gen Francis D, GOC, Berlin (British Sector), 1956-59

Rose, E Michael, Counsellor, FO, 1955-60; Minister, British Embassy, Bonn, 1960-63

Rostow, Walt W, Assistant to Secretary, UN Economic Commission for Europe, 1947-49; Deputy Special Assistant to the US President for National Security Affairs, 1961; Counsellor and Chair, Policy Planning Council, State Department, 1961-66

Rowan, Thomas L, PPS to the Prime Minister, 1941-47; Permanent Secretary, Office of Minister for Economic Affairs, 1947; Second Secretary, Treasury, 1947-49

Rowe-Ham, Sir David K, Lord Mayor, London, 1986-87; HM Lieutenant, City of London, 1987-2004

Royall, Kenneth C, US Under Secretary of War, 1945-47; Secretary of War, 1947; Secretary of the Army, 1947-49

Rühe, Volker, Deputy Chair, CDU/CSU Parliamentary Group, 1982-89; Secretary-General, CDU, 1989-91

Ruhnau, Heinz, Chairman, *Lufthansa*, 1982-91

Rumbold Sir Horace, AUS, FO, 1957-60; Minister, British Embassy, Paris, 1960-63

Rundall, Sir Francis, DUS (Chief Clerk), FO, 1959-63

Rusk, D Dean, US Secretary of State, 1961-69

Russell, John W, Counsellor, British Embassy, Tehran, 1956-59; Head, News Department, FO, 1959-62

Russell, Sir Mark, Chief Clerk, FCO, 1986-89

Ryder, Michael, Second, later First, Secretary, BMG Berlin, 1986-88; First Secretary, WED, 1988-93

Salvesen, C Hugh, First Secretary, British Embassy, Bonn, 1985-88; First Secretary, WED, 1988-93

Samuel, Adrian C I, PS to the Secretary of State for Foreign Affairs, 1959-63

Samuel, Sir Herbert, Leader of the Liberal Party, 1931-35

Sanders, Air Chief Marshal Sir Arthur, Air Officer Commanding, British Air Forces of Occupation, Germany, 1947-48; Vice-Chief of the Air Staff, 1948-50

Sands, Richard M, First Secretary (Economic) and Civil Air Attaché, British Embassy Bonn, 1985-89; First Secretary and Head of Chancery, British Embassy, East Berlin, 1989-90

Sandys, Duncan E, Minister of Aviation, 1959-60; Secretary of State for Commonwealth Relations, 1960-64

Saunders, Wing Commander Hugh W L, Air Officer C-in-C, Bomber Command, 1947; Air Council Member for Personnel, 1947-49; Inspector-General of the RAF, 1949-50

Schabowski, Günter, Secretary, SED Central Committee, 1986-89

Schalck-Golodkowski, Alexander, State-Secretary, Foreign Trade, GDR External Economics Ministry, 1975-89; member Economic Committee, SED Politburo, 1977-89

Schäuble, Wolfgang, Federal German Minister without Portfolio and Chief of the Federal Chancellery, 1984-89; Minister of the Interior, 1989-91

Scheel, Walter, Federal German President, 1974-79

Scherpenberg, Albert H van, State-Secretary, Federal German Foreign Ministry, 1958-61; Federal German Ambassador to the Holy See, 1961-64

Schertz, Georg, West Berlin Police President, 1987-90; Berlin Police President, 1990-92

Schmid, Prof Carlo, Deputy State President, Württemberg-Hohenzollern, 1947-48; member of Württemberg-Hohenzollern Parliamentary *Rathaus*, 1948-49; member of the *Bundestag*, 1949-72

Schnitzler, Karl-Eduard von, GDR commentator; presenter of 'Der schwarze Kanal', *Deutscher Fernsehfunk*, 1960-89

Scholz, Arno, Berlin journalist and publisher of the *Telegraf*; member, Berlin *Stadtverordnetenversammlung*, 1948-50

Scholz, Rupert, Senator for Justice, West Berlin, 1981-88; Senator for Federal Affairs, West Berlin, 1983-88; Federal German Defence Minister, 1988-90

Schramm, Hilde, West Berlin *Senat* deputy 1989; Deputy President, Berlin House of Representatives until March 1990

Schreyer, Michaele, member of the Green *Fraktion* and Senator for Development and Environmental Protection, Berlin, 1989-90

Schroeder, Louise D, acting *Oberbürgermeister*, Berlin, 1947-48

Schröder, Professor Dieter, State-Secretary, Head of the Federal German Senate Chancellery, Berlin, 1989-90

Schumacher, Kurt, Chairman, SPD, 1946-52

Schwennicke, Carl-Hubert, LDP member, Berlin House of Representatives, 1946-58

Schuman, Robert, French Foreign Minister, 1948-53

Schwierzina, Tino-Antoni, *Oberbürgermeister*, East Berlin, 1990-91

Scott, Sir Robert H, Commandant, Imperial Defence College, 1960-61

Scott-Barrett, Maj-Gen David W, British GOC, Berlin, 1973-75

Seal, Eric, Director-General, Building Materials, Ministry of Works, 1947-48; DUS, FO (German Section), 1948-51

Seebohm, Hans-Christoph, Minister for Reconstruction and Work, Lower Saxony, 1947-48; member, parliamentary *Rathaus*, Lower Saxony, 1948-49; member of the *Bundestag*, 1949-67

Seiters, Rudolf, Senior Parliamentary Manager, CDU/CSU, *Bundestag*, 1984-89; German Federal Minister without Portfolio and Head of Federal Chancellery, 1989-91

Seitz, Raymond G H, Deputy Chief of Mission, US Embassy, London, 1984-89; Assistant Secretary for European and Canadian Affairs, State Department, 1989-91

Serpell, David R, Principal, Treasury, 1945-54; Under-Secretary, Treasury, 1954-60; Deputy Secretary, Department of Transport, 1960-63

Shawcross, Sir Hartley W, Attorney-General, 1945-51

Shevardnadze, Eduard A, Soviet Foreign Minister, 1985-91

Shikin, Gennadi S, Soviet Ambassador, Vienna, 1986-90; Soviet Ambassador, East Berlin, 1990

Shinwell, Emanuel, Secretary of State for War, 1947-50

Shostal, Pierre, Director, Office of Central European Affairs, US State Department, 1987-90

Shuckburgh, Sir Evelyn, Assistant Secretary-General, NATO, 1958-60; DUS, FO, 1960-63

Shultz, George P, US Secretary of State, 1982-89

Siddle John, Legal Adviser, British Embassy, Bonn, 1984-87; Legal Counsellor, FCO, 1987-90

Simmons, Robert F, Jnr, Political Officer, US Mission to NATO, Brussels, 1989-93

Sinclair, Ian MacTaggart, Legal Adviser, British Embassy, Bonn, 1957-60; Assistant Legal Adviser, FO, 1960-64

Slater, Duncan, AUS, FCO, 1986-92

Smirnov, Andrei A, Soviet Deputy Minister of Foreign Affairs, 1946-49; Ambassador, Bonn, 1957-66

Smith, Frederick, Deputy Director, Cereals, Shipping and Statistics Section, German Supply Department, FO, 1948-49

Smith, Roland H, Head of Chancery, BMG Berlin, 1984-88

Smith, Gen Walter Bedell, US Ambassador, Moscow, 1946-49

Smith, Howard Kingsbury, American journalist, CBS Chief European Correspondent, London, 1946-57; news commentator, ABC, Washington, 1957-61

Snetkov, Gen Boris V, Commander, Soviet forces in the GDR, 1987-90

Soames, A Christopher J, Secretary of State for War, 1958-60; Minister of Agriculture, Fisheries and Food, 1960-64

Sokolovsky, Marshal Vasilii D, Chief of the Soviet Military Administration for Germany and Soviet Representative on the Allied Control Commission for Germany, 1946-49

Soldatov, Aleksandr A, Senior Counsellor, Soviet Delegation to the UN and Representative on the Trusteeship Council, 1948-53; Ambassador, London, 1960-66

Soskice, Frank, Solicitor-General, 1945-51

Spaak, Paul-Henri, Secretary-General, NATO, 1957-61; Belgian Deputy Prime Minister and Minister of Foreign and African Affairs, 1961-66

Speaight, Richard L, Counsellor and Head, IPD, FO, 1948-50

Spencer, Rosemary J, Head of ECD(E), FCO, 1987-89; AUS (Public Departments), FCO, 1989-92

Staffelt, Ditmar, Deputy Chairman, SPD *Fraktion*, Berlin House of Representatives, 1985-89; Chairman, 1989-94

Stagg, C Richard V, First Secretary, UKREP Brussels, 1987-88; First Secretary, FCO, 1988-91

Stahmer, Ingrid, *Bürgermeisterin* and Senator for Health and Social Issues, West Berlin, 1989-91

Stalin, Generalissimo Josef V, President of the Council of Ministers of the Soviet Union, 1946-53

Stapleton, Group Capt Deryck C, Secretary, Chiefs of Staff Committee, MoD, 1947-49; Plans, Bomber Command HQ, 1957-60; Air Ministry, 1960-62

Steel, Christopher E, Head, Political Division, Control Commission for Germany (British Element), 1945-47; President of the Governmental Sub-Commission and Political Adviser, 1947-49; Deputy High Commissioner, Germany, 1949-50; British Ambassador, Bonn, 1957-63

Steinhoff, Karl, GDR Interior Minister, 1949-52

Stephenson, Sir Hugh S, Consul-General, New York, 1957-60; DUS, FO, 1960-63

Stevens, (later Sir) Roger, Counsellor, FO, 1946-48; AUS, FO, 1948-51; DUS, FO, 1958-63

Stewart, B H Ian H, Minister of State for the Armed Forces, MoD, 1987-88

Stikker, Dirk U, Netherlands Permanent Representative to NATO and to Council of OEEC, Paris, 1958-61

Stolpe, Manfred, Consistorial President, eastern region of the Evangelical Church of Berlin-Brandenburg and member, Conference of the Governing Bodies of the Evangelical Churches in the GDR, 1982-90; Deputy Chairman, Federation of Evangelical Churches, 1982-89

Stoltenberg, Gerhard, Federal German Defence Minister, 1989-92

Strachey, E John StL, Minister of Food, 1946-50

Strang, Sir William, PUS, FO (German Section), 1947-49; PUS, FO, 1949-53

Stratton, Richard J, First Secretary, British Embassy, Bonn, 1958-60

Strauss, Franz-Josef, Federal German Minister of Defence, 1956-62

Strauss, George, Minister of Supply, 1947-51

Streibl, Max, Bavarian Minister-President, 1988-93

Strong, Sir Kenneth W D, Director-General, PID, FO, 1945-47; First Director of Joint Intelligence Bureau, MoD, 1948-64

Sudhoff, Jürgen, State-Secretary, Federal German Foreign Ministry, 1987-91

Suhr, Otto, Chairman, Berlin City Assembly; member of the National Executive Committee of the SPD, 1948

Synnott, Hilary N H, Head, WED, FCO, 1989-91

Szatmari, Istvan, Hungarian Minister-Counsellor, East Berlin, 1989

Tait, Michael L, AUS (Soviet Union and Eastern Europe), 1990-92

Tedder, Marshal Arthur W, Lord, Chief of the Air Staff and First and Senior Air Member, Air Council, 1946-50

Teltschik, Horst, Head of Department 41 (Foreign and Inner German Relations), Federal German Chancellery office, 1982-91

Templer, Gerald W R, Lt-Gen, Director, Military Intelligence, War Office, 1946-48; Vice-Chief of the Imperial General Staff, 1948-50

Thape, Ernst, Minister of Education, Science and Culture, Saxony-Anhalt, 1946-48

Thatcher, Margaret H, MP for Finchley, 1959-92; Minister of Pensions and National Insurance, 1961-64; Prime Minister, 1979-90

Thedieck, Franz, State-Secretary, Federal German Ministry of All-German Affairs, 1949-64

Thompson, Llewellyn E, US Ambassador, Moscow, 1957-62

Thomson, John A, PS to the PUS, FO, 1958-60; First Secretary, British Embassy, Washington, 1960-64

Thorneycroft, G E Peter, Minister of Aviation, 1960-62

Timsit, Joelle, French Ambassador, East Berlin, 1986-90

Tisch, Harry, GDR Free German Trade Union Federation Chairman, 1975-89

Tito, Marshal Josip Broz, Yugoslav Prime Minister and Minister of National Defence, 1945-1980

Tomkins, Edward E, Head, Western Department, FO, 1959-63

Tomkys, W Roger, AUS and Principal Finance Officer, FCO, 1987-89; DUS, 1989-90

Tomlinson, Frank S, British Deputy Commandant, Berlin, 1959-61; Deputy Permanent UK Representative, NATO, 1961-64

Tomlinson, George, Minister of Education, 1947-51

Touré, A Sekou, President, Republic of Guinea, 1958-84; Prime Minister, 1958-72

Truman, Harry S, US President, 1945-53

Trupiano, Francesco P, Counsellor, Italian Mission to NATO, Brussels, 1985-90

Tschöppe, Armin, State-Secretary, Department of Health and Social Affairs, Berlin *Senat*, 1989

Tucker, Andrew V G, First Secretary and Press Attaché, British Embassy, Moscow 1987-90

Tulpanov, Col Alexander, Head, Soviet Information Services, Berlin, 1948

Tunner, Lt-Gen William H, Commander, Atlantic Division, US Military Air Transport Service (director of Berlin airlift), 1948-49

Ulbricht, Walter, General Secretary, SED, 1950-71; GDR Chairman of the Council of State, 1960-73

Vandenberg, Gen Hoyt S, USAF Chief of Staff, 1948-53

Vaugier, Georges M J, Deputy Director for Central and Northern Europe, French Foreign Ministry, 1986-90; First Counsellor, French Embassy, Washington, 1990-93

Vinson, Frederick M, US Chief Justice, 1946-53

Vogel, Hans-Jochen, *Regierender Bürgermeister*, West Berlin, 1981; Chair, SPD Parliamentary Party, 1984-91; Deputy Chair, SPD, 1984-87; Chair, SPD, 1987-90

Voroshilov, Marshal Kliment Y, member, CPSU Politburo, 1926-61; Chairman, Presidium of the Supreme Soviet, 1953-60

Vyshinsky, Andrei Y, Soviet Deputy Minister for Foreign Affairs, 1940-49; Minister for Foreign Affairs, 1949-53

Waffenschmidt, Horst, Parliamentary State-Secretary, Federal German Interior Ministry, 1982-97

Wagner, Horst, Berlin Senator for Work, Transport and Business, 1989-91

Waigel, Theodor, Federal German Minister of Finance, 1989-98

Waldegrave, William A, Minister of State for Housing, Department of the Environment, 1987-88; Minister of State, FCO, 1988-90; Secretary of State for Health, 1990-92

Walker, C Michael, Principal, Dominions Office, 1947-49; First Secretary, British Embassy, Washington, 1949-51

Wall, J Stephen, PPS to the Secretary of State for Foreign and Commonwealth Affairs, 1988-91

Walters, Lt-Gen Vernon A, US Permanent Representative to the UN, 1985-89; US Ambassador, Bonn, 1989-91

Ward, George F, Jnr, Political-military officer, US State Department, 1985-88; Deputy Chief of Mission, US Embassy, Bonn, 1989-92

Waterfield, Lt-Col P R M, COS Secretariat, 1946-49

Watkinson, Harold A, Minister of Transport and Civil Aviation, 1955-59; Minister of Defence, 1959-62

Watson, Maj-Gen Albert, US Commandant, Berlin, 1961-63

Watts, Sir Arthur D, Legal Adviser, FCO, 1987-91

Webb, Simon, Head, Agency Team, MoD, 1989; PS to Secretary of State for Defence, MoD, 1989-92

Wechmar, Baron Rüdiger von, Federal German Ambassador, London, 1985-89

Wedemeyer, Lt-Gen Albert C, Director of Plans and Operations, US Department of the Army, General Staff, 1947-48; Deputy Chief of Staff for Plans, Office of Chief of Staff, 1948-49

Weeks, Lt-Gen Sir Ronald M, Deputy Governor and Chief of Staff, British Zone, CCG, 1945

Weir, Sir Cecil McA, President, Economic Sub-Commission, CCG (British Element) and Economic Adviser to the BMG Berlin, 1946-49

Weizsäcker, Richard von, *Regierender Bürgermeister*, West Berlin, 1981-84; Federal German President, 1984-94

Weston, P John, DUS (Defence), FCO, 1989-90; Political Director and DUS (Europe), FCO, 1990-91

Weygandt, Arkell D, International Transportation and Communications Officer, US Embassy, Bonn, 1988-92

Whitehead, John C, US Deputy Secretary of State, 1985-89

Whiteley, William, Parliamentary Secretary to the Treasury, 1945-51

Whitting, Ian R, Second Secretary (Commercial), British Embassy, Moscow, 1985-88; Second Secretary, FCO, 1988-90; First Secretary, British Embassy, Dublin, 1990-94

Wilding, Richard W L, Second Secretary, FO, 1957-59; Principal, Treasury, 1959-67

Wilkinson, Peter A, Counsellor, British Embassy, Bonn, 1955-60; Head, PUSD, 1960-63

Williams, Michael S, Minister, British Embassy, Bonn, 1956-60

Williams, Thomas, Minister of Agriculture and Fisheries, 1945-51

Williams, Air Vice Marshal Thomas M, Commandant, RAF Staff College, 1947-48; C-in-C, BAFO, 1948-51

Williams, James A, Deputy Assistant Chief of Mission, US Mission, West Berlin, 1986-90

Wilms, Dorothee, Federal German Minister for German Affairs, 1987-91

Wilson, J Harold, Parliamentary Secretary to the Board of Works, 1945-47; Secretary for Overseas Trade, 1947; President of the Board of Trade, 1947-51; Prime Minister, 1964-70 and 1974-76

Wohlrabe, Jürgen, President, Berlin House of Representatives, 1989-91

Wolf, Christa (Christa Ihlenfeld), GDR author and literary critic

Wolf, Markus J, Head of General Reconnaissance Division, GDR State Security Ministry, 1953-86

Wood, Andrew M, British Ambassador, Belgrade, 1985-89; Minister, British Embassy, Washington, 1989-92

Wood, Michael C, Legal Counsellor, FCO, 1986-91

Woodburn, Arthur, Secretary of State for Scotland, 1947-50

Woods, Ian A, Second Secretary, British Embassy, Bonn, 1986-89; First Secretary, later Counsellor, FCO, 1989-95

Wordsworth, Stephen J, First Secretary, WED, 1988-90; First Secretary (Political), British Embassy, Bonn, 1990-94

Wright, Sir Patrick R H, PUS, FCO, 1986-91

Wronski, Edmund, Berlin Senator for Transport and Business, 1985-89

Yakovlev, Alexander N, economist and adviser to Mikhail Gorbachev; member, CPSU Politburo, 1987-90

Yarnold, Patrick, Head, Defence Department, FCO, 1987-90; British Consul-General, Hamburg, 1990-94

Zaikov, Lev N, member, CPSU Politburo, 1986-90; First Secretary, Moscow Communist Party, 1987-89

Zakharov, Matvei V, Soviet Commandant, Berlin, 1958-61

Zaroubin, Georgii N, Soviet Ambassador, London, 1947-52

Zimmermann, Friedrich, Federal German Interior Minister, 1982-89; Transport Minister, 1989-91

Zorin, Valerian A, Soviet Deputy Minister of Foreign Affairs, 1947-55

Zulueta, Philip F de, PS to the Prime Minister, 1955-64

CHAPTER I

Berlin Isolated 1948-1949

The 'fate' of Berlin was, in the words of the British Prime Minister, Harold Wilson, 'a touchstone of the state of relations in Europe'.[1] In his opening address to the third and final stage of the Conference on Security and Cooperation in Europe (CSCE) in Helsinki on 30 July 1975, a symbolic highpoint in an era of East-West détente, Wilson thus reminded assembled delegates of a city whose recent history was far more closely entwined with the fortunes of a divided continent than was that of the Finnish capital. That Berlin had come to occupy this position was due to: (*a*) the decisions made by the British, Soviet and United States Governments during the latter stages of the Second World War on the division of Germany into zones and of Berlin into sectors; (*b*) post-war differences amongst the former allies over the future of Germany and the transformation of the American, British and French sectors of Berlin into what amounted to a Western enclave within the Soviet zone; and (*c*) the onset of the Cold War and the emergence of two separate German states. The rights of the four occupying powers derived from Germany's unconditional surrender and their joint assumption of supreme authority in respect of Germany. In the immediate aftermath of the war a Control Council for Germany was established, whose function was to ensure uniformity of action by Commanders-in-Chief in their respective zones, and under its general direction a four-power *Kommandatura* assumed responsibility for the administration of Greater Berlin, a territory extending over 344 square miles. Sector boundaries were defined by the *Kommandatura*, the city's postal system was reorganised, and a special committee was established to complete the organisation for the provisioning of the population. Meanwhile, at a meeting of the Allied High Command on 25 June 1945 an informal provisional compromise was agreed on traffic rights through the Soviet zone. This provided the three Western powers with access to Berlin via a long-distance highway, one railway and two air routes.

Allied efforts to restore some semblance of representative civilian government in Berlin proved more problematic. The failure of the predominantly communist Socialist Unity Party (*Sozialistische Einheitspartei Deutschlands* (SED)) to win more than 19.8 per cent of the popular vote in City Assembly elections in October 1946 set the Soviet authorities on a collision course with the majority Social Democrats. The Russians resisted attempts to replace communist officials in the city administration, and in June 1947 they vetoed the Assembly's election of Ernst Reuter as *Oberbürgermeister* (Lord Mayor). Yet of equal consequence for Berlin's future were the divisions emerging between the former wartime allies. The Moscow meeting of the Council of Foreign Ministers (CFM) of March-April 1947 coincided with the enunciation of the Truman Doctrine and was characterised more by rising East-West tensions than by progress towards a German settlement. Meanwhile, with a view to revitalising the German economy, the British and US Governments proceeded towards the economic unification of their two zones in western Germany. An Economic Council was created, consisting of German representatives from each of the *Länder* of this 'Bizonia', with responsibility for adopting and

[1] Cmnd. 6932, *Selected Documents relating to Problems of Security and Cooperation in Europe, 1954-77* (London: HMSO, 1977), p. 218.

promulgating ordinances subject to approval by an Anglo-American bipartite board.[2] By November Washington was contemplating the extension to Germany of the economic assistance initially offered by the US Secretary of State, George C Marshall, for the economic revival of Europe. Indeed, when the subsequent London sessions of the CFM proved as politically fruitless as those previously held in Moscow, Marshall and the British Foreign Secretary, Ernest Bevin, agreed on the need for currency reform in Germany and on the possible strengthening of the bizonal administrative structure through the holding of direct elections for the Economic Council.[3]

Discussions in Frankfurt-am-Main on 7-8 January 1948 between the British and US Military Governors for Germany, the bizonal authorities, and the Ministers-President of the *Länder*, were followed by legislation on 9 February for the revision of the bizonal German Economic Administration and the creation of a bizonal German High Court, and on 14 February for the establishment of a German central bank.[4] The Russians wasted no time in condemning these moves. When at a meeting of the Control Council on 20 January, General Lucius D Clay, the US Military Governor, reported on the understanding reached at Frankfurt, Marshal Vasilii Sokolovsky, his Soviet opposite number, responded with a statement to the effect that the British and US Governments had 'taken a new step towards the splitting of Germany and the establishment of a Western German State' in violation of the Potsdam Agreement.[5] A meeting in London from 23 February to 6 March of American, British, French and Benelux representatives to discuss German affairs further provoked Soviet ire, especially following the issue of a preliminary communiqué recommending a federal form of government for Western Germany with a corresponding central authority as the first stage towards a later reunification.[6] On 20 March Sokolovsky, after a bitter exchange of views with his Western colleagues, stormed out of the allied Control Council in Berlin, effectively terminating the Council's work (No. 5). Meanwhile, an alternative communist-inspired political structure began to take shape with the SED's summoning of a German People's Congress for Unity and a Just Peace and the subsequent formation of a German People's Council (*Deutscher Volksrat*). A communist coup in Prague on 25 February, and the signing on 17 March of the Brussels Treaty, linking Britain, France, Belgium, Luxembourg and the Netherlands in a collective defence pact, were likewise evidence of the deepening ideological rift between Eastern and Western Europe. Prior to the reconvening of the six-power London Conference on 20 April the French, who had hitherto been reluctant to accept measures which they feared would lead to a powerful centralised German government, agreed tentatively to the merger of their zone of Germany with those of Britain and the United States. They also eventually accepted the recommendations of the Conference, which concluded its deliberations on 1 June, for the summoning of a constituent assembly.[7] Then, on 20 June 1948, after some hesitation on the French part, the three Western occupying powers proceeded with the implementation in

[2] *Foreign Relations of the United States (FRUS) 1947*, vol. ii, pp. 909-77.

[3] *Ibid.*, pp. 811-29.

[4] *FRUS 1948*, vol. ii, pp. 4-16 and 59-60.

[5] Berlin telegram No. 111 of 20 January 1948, C 506/71/18). See Series I, Volume I, No. 603.

[6] *FRUS 1948*, vol. ii, pp. 75-145.

[7] *Ibid.*, pp. 191-337.

their zones (but not initially in their sectors of Berlin) of a currency reform—a move generally regarded as having triggered the first major crisis over Berlin.

A War of Nerves, 10 January–29 April 1948

An inter-allied crisis over Berlin was not unexpected. Clay had predicted in November 1947 that the implementation of plans for a unified West German administration would be accompanied by an early effort on the part of the Russians to blockade the city and drive out the Western occupying powers.[8] No such measures were in the first instance taken directly against British, French or US authorities in Berlin. Yet, as the documents in this section reveal, both in their dealings with the *Magistrat*, Berlin's executive council, and with the leaders and officials of non-communist parties, the Russians seemed increasingly ready to engage in acts which General Sir Brian Robertson, the British Military Governor for Germany and Commander-in-Chief in Berlin, considered indicative of 'the intense war of nerves ... against the Germans' (No. 1). There was, in consequence, great anxiety in the city lest the Western allies should withdraw, and while in Robertson's opinion few Germans doubted their wish to maintain their position, many were uncertain about their ability to do so in the face of Soviet pressure (No. 2). Events in Prague and restrictions imposed by the Russians on communications between Berlin and the Western zones in the wake of Sokolovsky's departure from the Control Council only added to German fears. And while Bevin was determined that Britain 'must stay' in Berlin, he was well aware of the West's vulnerability to Soviet pressure (Nos. 3-6). 'There is nowhere in the world', Bevin observed, 'where we can make difficulties for the Russians in the same way as they can make difficulties for the Western Powers in Berlin without risk of serious damage to ourselves' (No. 7).

Nor could Robertson think of a good way in which the Western powers could retaliate in Germany. Their legal position with regard to Berlin was, he admitted, 'weak'. As he explained in a telegram of 2 April, 'the original agreement which set up Berlin as an island in the Soviet zone without assured means of communication to other zones' had been concluded on the assumption that the Russians would remain allies and friends, and subsequent agreements had likewise been informal and unrecorded in writing. The main object of the Russians was, he thought, 'to screw the iron curtain down more firmly', but, he added, they were also seeking to demonstrate that they had the other occupying powers 'by the throat' and that they could 'close their fingers whenever they [felt] inclined to do so' (No. 8). Yet, while Robertson was prepared to contemplate some agreement with the Russians on their inspection of rail traffic with the Western zones, his American colleague was not. Clay, in Robertson's words, was 'pessimistic and bellicose' and 'quite adamant against any form of compromise' (No. 9). If the Russians were to attempt to use force, then, Robertson predicted, Clay, with Washington's approval, 'would treat this as an act of war'. In such circumstances Robertson and senior officials in London concluded that the best course for Britain was 'to "sit it out" and to say as little as possible' (No. 12). Soviet tactics suggested that they were pursuing a deliberate plan of gradual encroachments aimed at undermining the Western position in Berlin, while at the same time avoiding a direct challenge which might involve the risk of war. The danger, in Robertson's estimate, was that once the Russians were wholly satisfied that the ground was fully prepared and their

[8] L D Clay, *Germany and the Fight for Freedom* (Cambridge, Mass.: Harvard University Press, 1950), p. 36.

propaganda case established, they would seek to forestall Anglo-American plans for currency reform and the establishment of a West German government by 'decisive steps in Berlin and the Soviet Zone' (No. 13).

DOCUMENT SUMMARIES

	DOCUMENT	DATE	MAIN SUBJECT
1	Berlin tel 49 C 218/3/18	**1948** 10 Jan	Reports on signs of increasing Soviet war of nerves directed at Germans in Berlin.
2	Berlin tel 178 C 871/3/18	3 Feb	Notes German anxiety lest Western allies withdraw from Berlin.
3	Berlin tel 336 C 1727/3/18	3 Mar	Assesses impact on opinion in Berlin of communist takeover in Czechoslovakia.
4	Minute: Strang to Bevin C 2319/3/18	18 Mar	Argues that allies must stay in Berlin; and suggests practical steps to improve their position and German morale.
5	Berlin tel 434 C 2211/71/18	20 Mar	Reports on Soviet delegation's withdrawal from Control Council.
6	Berlin tel 494 C 2473/3/18	31 Mar	Considers new Soviet restrictions on E-W rail traffic a serious development foreshadowing further squeeze on allied communications.
7	Tel 652 to Berlin C 2473/3/18	1 Apr	Agrees with No. 6, and asks how allies can 'hit the Russians without harming ourselves?'
8	Berlin tel 510 C 2529/3/18	2 Apr	Interim reply to No. 7: Military Governor 'can think of no good retaliation within Germany'.
9	Berlin tel 519 C 2543/3/18	2 Apr	Reports that US Governor's attitude to Berlin situation is 'most pessimistic and bellicose'.
10	Berlin tel 525 C 2553/3/18	2 Apr	Notes Soviet press justification for tightening of traffic control: 'masses of spies' from British/US zones.
11	Tel 659 to Berlin C 2529/3/18	2 Apr	Urges need for a *modus vivendi* and recommends a firm but calm reaction if the Russians overstep the mark.
12	Minute: Strang to Bevin C 3580/3/18	24 Apr	Attaches record of meeting on British policy in Berlin: in response to increased Soviet

			pressure 'we should say nothing and simply stay put'.
13	Berlin tel 776 C 3662/3/18	29 Apr	Reports that Soviets were deliberately undermining Western position in Berlin while avoiding direct challenge.
14	Despt 632 to Washington C 3418/3/18	29 Apr	Reports Bevin's advice to US Ambassador to delay approach to Soviet Govt: the problem was wider than Berlin alone.

The Crisis breaks, 19-30 June 1948

During May and early June 1948 the Soviet authorities continued, slowly but surely, to tighten their grip on communications between Berlin and the Western zones. Barge traffic was virtually suspended, as were parcel post and export traffic from the West. Trains from the West were held up or turned back, and the Elbe Bridge on the Autobahn between Berlin and the West was 'closed for repairs'. The work of the *Kommandatura* was brought almost to a standstill by Soviet tactics of obstruction and dilatoriness. However, discussions between British, French and US financial experts on currency reform for the Western zones continued and, despite difficult negotiations, a scheme for the introduction of a new Deutsche Mark currency and the cancellation or blocking of old Reichsmark holdings and debts was hammered out during May and accepted by both Western governments and German representatives. Sokolovsky, who was formally informed of the impending currency reform on 18 June,[9] responded swiftly. In a public proclamation, he condemned the move as a 'heavy blow struck against the constitutional unity of Germany', implemented by Western 'monopolists' with the aim of weakening and subjugating the German economy. The circulation of the new notes was forbidden both in the Soviet zone and in Greater Berlin which, Sokolovsky claimed, formed 'part of the Soviet Occupation Zone from the economic point of view', and further travel restrictions were promulgated, including the suspension of train passenger services into and out of the Soviet zone (Nos. 15 & 16).

A meeting held at Clay's invitation on 22 June between financial experts of the four occupying powers failed to reach agreement on the currency situation in Berlin. The Russians rejected both Western proposals for a separate Berlin currency and the suggestion that, if Berlin retained the same currency as the surrounding Soviet zone, there should be four-power control over issuance and credit policies for the city. And, following the announcement on 23 June of a currency reform for the Soviet zone and Berlin, the British, French and US Military Governors declared that the new Deutsche Mark would be extended to their sectors. There it would circulate alongside the new Soviet zone currency, which would be treated as legal tender. The Soviet authorities countered with a fresh raft of measures evidently intended to intimidate Berliners and, early on the morning of 24 June, they announced that all rail traffic between Berlin and the Western zones and all electricity supplies from the Eastern to the Western sectors would be halted (Nos. 16 & 17). Quite what Soviet objectives were remained uncertain. As Hector McNeil, Minister of State at the Foreign Office, pointed out in a preliminary assessment of

[9] For the text of General Robertson's letter to Sokolovsky see Cmd. 7534, *An account of the events leading up to a reference of the Berlin question to the United Nations* (London: HMSO, 11 October 1948), p. 17.

24 June, it was impossible to say whether the Russians were intent on forcing the Western allies out of Berlin, or whether the latest measures were the 'first step in establishing a strong negotiating position for an eventual bargain between the Four Powers on Berlin in particular and Germany as a whole' (No. 18). And while the Russians had taken up a position from which it would be difficult to retreat, they had, Robertson explained in a telegram of 25 June, by making no formal demand for the Western allies' departure and by not excluding the possibility of the Control Council and the *Kommandatura* resuming their functions, 'left themselves a line of retreat in case of necessity' (No. 23). Nonetheless, despite protest notes sent to Sokolovsky by the British, French and US Military Governors (No. 25), it rapidly became clear that the Berlin problem could not be resolved simply on a local basis.

Bevin was as determined as ever that the Western allies should remain in Berlin. If they were forced out in 'humiliating circumstances', then he feared the effects would be 'extremely grave not only in Berlin but in Western Germany and in Europe at large' (No. 27). Plans for a Western Union defence organisation based on the Brussels Treaty might then, he told the Cabinet, be 'fatally weakened' (No. 31). He was therefore anxious to ensure the fullest allied cooperation and particularly the backing of the US Chiefs of Staff. Moreover, he wanted as large as possible a force of aircraft to encourage morale in Berlin, and the 'provision of a large bomber force' with which to deter the Soviet Government from attempting to drive out the Western allies (No. 27). Both the British and American Chiefs of Staff were, however, agreed that it would be impracticable to force convoys through to Berlin by rail or road, though they were ready to contemplate shooting down barrage balloons that the Russians might put up to obstruct air corridors (No. 32). For the moment, the main effort was to be put into increasing food stocks for the civilian population of the Western sectors. The US Air Force was already transporting 1,000 tons a day by air into their sector (No. 31), and the British hoped to lift 750 tons by air after 3 July (No. 32). But, as Bevin told a meeting of the ministerial committee on Germany on 28 June, to maintain the population in the three Western sectors of Berlin on their present scale of rations, a daily lift of the order of 2,000 tons would be required (No. 35).

Despite the logistical problems resulting from the intensification of the Soviet blockade of the Western sectors of Berlin, Bevin remained confident that war could be avoided (No. 33). A retreat would, he thought, be 'disastrous'. It would lead to a collapse of confidence in Western Germany, the 'collapse of our whole Western system', and 'the complete domination of Europe by Russia reinforced by a Communist controlled Germany'. He was likewise opposed to any idea of the Western powers negotiating with the Russians on the basis of the Declaration emanating from a meeting in Warsaw on 23-24 June of the Foreign Ministers of the Soviet Union and its East European satellites. It demanded the complete demilitarisation of Germany, four-power control of the Ruhr, the establishment of an all-German provisional government, the fulfilment of German reparations commitments, and the conclusion of a peace treaty to be followed by the withdrawal of all occupation forces within a year of signature.[10] Bevin took the view that this 'was a statement on the fundamental policy of the Soviet Government' which the Russians hoped to use as the agenda for a further meeting of the CFM, and that 'it was designed to test the position of the Western Powers in the hope [they] would be found to be weakening on the German problem' (Nos. 36 & 37).

[10] *The Annual Register. A Review of Public Events at Home and Abroad for the Year 1948*, ed. I S Macadam (London: Longmans, Green and Co, 1949), pp. 240-41.

'We are', he told the Commons on 30 June, 'willing to have four-Power control, but we are not willing to have a façade of four-Power control, and one-Power direction.'[11] He was, in any case, keen to negotiate from a position of strength. He was thus reluctant to pursue an American idea for the despatch of a three-power note to Moscow asserting the rights of the Western allies in Berlin 'until the proposals for increasing the air lift ... and the bomber force were more advanced' (No. 36). A letter from Sokolovsky to Robertson of 29 June, which insisted on the temporary nature of the restrictions imposed on traffic between Berlin and the Western zones, required an answer (Nos. 45 & 46). And, for the moment, Bevin preferred to concentrate upon promoting Western solidarity, whilst leaving contacts with the Russians on Berlin to the Military Governors in Germany (No. 48).

DOCUMENT SUMMARIES

	DOCUMENT	DATE	SUBJECT
15	Berlin tel 1117 C 4798/4794/18	**1948** 19 June	Records Soviet denunciation of currency reforms in the Western zones.
16	Berlin tel 1118 C 4799/4794/18	19 June	Reports Soviet announcement of travel restrictions, introduced in response to currency reform in the West.
17	Cabinet Conclusions (extract) CAB 128/13	24 June	Notes serious situation in Berlin: Military Governor had been asked for full report by noon.
18	MacNeil to Attlee C 5093/3/18	24 June	Encloses full preliminary assessment of situation in Berlin based on Military Governor's reports.
19	Berlin tel 1162 C 4921/3/18	24 June	Summarises stock position: no reason to disguise seriousness of situation in Berlin.
20	Berlin tel 1166 C 4938/3/18	24 June	Details transport situation affecting Berlin.
21	Cabinet Conclusions (extract) CAB 128/13	25 June	Records agreement to set up ministerial committee: Minister of Defence to consider supplies for civil population; and Bevin to concert with France and the US.
22	Note by Kirkpatrick C 5095/3/18	25 June	Argues that Berlin problem can only be resolved at a governmental level.
23	Berlin tel 1180 C 5001/3/18	25 June	Maintains that Soviet tactics are rough, but leave a line of retreat.
24	Despt 914 to Washington	25 June	Records views expressed by Bevin to US Ambassador on Berlin

[11] Extract from House of Commons Debates, 30 June 1948, C 5231/3/18.

	C 5031/3/18		crisis, and proposals for military coordination.
25	Berlin tel 1189 C 4985/3/18	26 June	Text of communication from Robertson to be delivered to Sokolovsky at 11.30 a.m. calling for immediate restoration of normal traffic to and from Berlin.
26	Minute: Strang to Bevin C 5176/3/18	26 June	Recommends that supplies be sent to maintain morale, but cautions 'we could not feed 2 million people by air'.
27	Letter: Kirkpatrick to Hollis C 5015/3/18	26 June	Seeks Chiefs of Staff's views on situation, drawing attention to 'extreme political importance of maintaining our position in Berlin'.
28	MoD tel DOTEL 926 to BJSM Washington DEFE 11/321	26 June	Warns Joint Staff Mission they may be required to engage US Chiefs of Staff on Berlin at short notice.
29	Intel 257 to selected Posts CAB 21/1885	26 June	Quotes official statements regarding British determination to stay in Berlin.
30	Berlin tel 1199 C 5010/3/18	27 June	Reports discussions with Brownjohn and Clay about Berlin and possibility of increasing allied military resources.
31	Cabinet Conclusions (extract) CAB 128/13	28 June	Update on Berlin: Bevin says 'There could be no question of yielding to Soviet pressure.'
32	Minutes: COS (48) 88th mtg, Confidential Annex CAB 53/3	28 June	Records meeting with Director, Plans & Operations Staff, US Army, regarding air supply of Berlin and joint planning.
33	Record of informal meeting: Bevin/Noel-Baker/Commonwealth High Commissioners FO 800/467	28 June	Bevin reviews German situation: he is convinced that danger of war can be averted by standing firm on Berlin.
34	MOD tel COS (W) 585 to BJSM Washington C 5340/3/18	28 June	COS review military measures to hold position in Berlin and keep supplies flowing.
35	Minutes: GEN 241/1st mtg C 5136/3/18	28 June	Cabinet ministerial committee on Germany considers Berlin situation and measures needed.
36	Despt 924 to Washington C 5138/3/18	28 June	Records Bevin's communication of GEN 241 Cttee decisions to US Ambassador, and the latter's

			agreement that purpose of Warsaw Declaration is to delay Western programme in Germany.
37	Tel 1966 to Paris C 5135/3/18	28 June	Kirkpatrick briefs Oliver Harvey on Cabinet view that 'retreat would be disastrous' on Berlin and urges him to 'infuse courage into the French'.
38	Note by Strang C 5448/3/18	29 June	Records meeting between Bevin and Douglas: US Cabinet approval to be sought for recommendations based on 'We stay in Berlin'.
39	Note: Hollis to Murrie DEFE 11/321	29 June	Asserts that with a full US/British airlift, German population and allied forces could be fed for limited period.
40	Tel 1375 to Berlin C 5178/3/18	29 June	Relates misgivings about No. 41.
41	Tel 1376 to Berlin C 5178/3/18	29 June	US instructions to Clay: early discussion with Sokolovsky desirable; basic problem 'seems not currency but quadripartite authority'.
42	Alexander (MoD) to Bevin DEFE 11/321	29 June	Reports airlift of 75 tons per day is going ahead and will be expanded to 400 tons in next 48 hours.
43	GEN 241/2nd mtg CAB 130/38	29 June	Discussion of US attitude: three-power consultations; access to Berlin; assembly of airlift; Bevin reluctant to see Berlin question raised in UNSC at present.
44	Berlin tel 1224 C 5145/3/18	29 June	Replies to No. 40: Robertson reports Clay's agreement on importance of quadripartite control.
45	Berlin tel 1229 C 5148/3/18	30 June	Comments on No. 46: it should be treated with reserve, but indicates Soviet preparation to withdraw from current position.
46	Berlin tel 1230 C 5150/3/18	30 June	Transmits text of letter from Sokolovsky, stating that Soviet restrictions on East-West traffic are 'temporary', and complaining of British counter-measures.
47	Tel 11820 BASIC to Frankfurt C 5148/3/18	30 June	Reports Bevin's agreement with views expressed in Nos. 44 and 45: must get airlift started.

48	Despt 740 to Paris C 5196/3/18	30 June	Records Bevin/Massigli talks on Berlin and wider issues; Bevin stresses importance of 'rapid united action' in Germany.

Propaganda, Publicity and Deception, June-August 1948

The documents in this group are intended to illustrate another dimension of the crisis. They show attempts by all parties to put their case to public opinion in their own countries and in Germany itself; and the process of bluff and counter-bluff by which East and West sought to persuade their opponents that the struggle for Berlin was not one they could win. For the British, Berlin was important because it formed part of a number of pressing issues faced by the Government in the summer of 1948. On a global level, continuing conflict between India and Pakistan over Kashmir, and the precarious nature of the truce negotiated on 11 June between Jewish and Arab forces in Palestine, were the cause of deep concern. More optimistically, but involving important issues of principle and of detail, significant discussions on European security, that were to culminate in the signature of the North Atlantic Treaty in 1949, were taking place in Washington. Talks were in the meantime proceeding on the allocation of aid under Marshall's European Recovery Programme (ERP), and plans were being made for a range of consultative bodies whose establishment had been agreed under the terms of the Brussels Treaty. Relations between the Western powers and the Soviet Union were fundamental to all these developments. But the Western position on Berlin was critical.

Bevin was particularly keen to give the utmost publicity to the British stance. Indeed, he sought to use the crisis both to strengthen the nascent Western alliance and to persuade Germans to identify with its aims and values. 'If we see this through, as we intend', he observed in a telegram to Berlin, 'it may have the fortunate result of implanting in the German mind a real sense of community and common purpose with the West' (No. 50). Propaganda directives were despatched to British officials throughout Germany, emphasising Soviet responsibility for the blockade of Berlin and the threatened starvation of more than two million of its citizens (Nos. 52, 54, 56 & 57). The British also tried their hand at military deception. Operation HATBAND was one such plan. This involved carrying out reconnaissance in West Germany in an attempt to give the Russians the impression that if a crisis erupted the British would be ready to reinforce the British Army of the Rhine (BAOR) with a home-based brigade (Nos. 51, 53 & 59). Soviet officers, meanwhile, attempted to ingratiate themselves with their British opposite numbers, and at a reception on 23 July Sokolovsky even went as far as to deny that there was any blockade of Berlin (Nos. 65 & 66). Food shortages in the city suggested otherwise. Anxiety amongst the people of Berlin about the winter was already beginning and fuel stocks were drastically low. And if the hardships and uncertainties created by the Soviet currency exchange were chiefly responsible for a serious drop in civilian morale, a 'little extra food would', in the words of one official, 'work wonders' (No. 68).

DOCUMENT SUMMARIES

	DOCUMENT	DATE	MAIN SUBJECT
49	Berlin tel 1220 C 5126/3/18	29 June	Argues pressure could be put on the Russians by 'the selective mobilisation of world opinion'.
50	Tel 1382 to Berlin C 5126/3/18	29 June	Expresses Bevin's desire for 'utmost publicity' of British policy and events in Berlin.
51	Letter: Hollis to Kirkpatrick DEFE 11/321	30 June	Informs that Hollis has asked COS to reconsider plan to deceive Russians by creating impression of reinforcement.
52	CCG(BE) tel BGCC 5112 to Regions CCG 215/2513	2 July	Propaganda Directive No. 1 for use in guidance to media in Germany and UK.
53	COS(48) 91st mtg: Confidential Annex DEFE 11/321	2 July	Discussion of troop reconnaissance in Germany: doubts about value of proposed deception.
54	CCG(BE) tel BGCC 5196 to Regions CCG 215/2513	5 July	Refers to No. 52: themes to be developed by all available means; Soviet responsibility for Berlin situation to be made clear.
55	Despt 239 to Berlin C 5439/3/18	6 July	Informs of Bevin's assurances to German Social Democrats that he will never abandon efforts to secure German unity.
56	Berlin tel 1338 CCG 215/977	9 July	Anticipates move of *Magistrat* and City Assembly to Western sectors: propaganda line will depend on course of events.
57	CCG(BE) tel BGCC 5411 to Regions CCG 215/2513	14 July	Sends publicity and propaganda material for implementation of instructions in No. 54.
58	Tel 1536 to Berlin CCG 215/2513	14 July	Transmits message of fraternal support from Parliamentary Labour Party to SDP, Berlin.
59	Hollis to COS CAB 21/1885	15 July	Reports visit to Germany by head of LCS and attaches deception plan 'Operation HATBAND'.
60	CCG(BE) Info Services Division tel 409 BASIC to Regions CCG 215/2513	16 July	Campaign Directive No 2: publicity information on Berlin economy and currency reform; owing to Soviet obstruction, economy of Berlin is not viable.

61	Tel 527 BASIC to Berlin CCG 215/2513	16 July	Refers to No. 57: argument in paragraph 11(*a*) 'will not hold water' and should be cancelled.
62	Tel 577 BASIC to Berlin CCG 215/2513	19 July	News guidance on Berlin: important to make disastrous consequences of withdrawal from Berlin 'absolutely clear'.
63	Moscow tel 851 CCG 215/2513	20 July	Reports Soviet press announcement of decision to place 100,000 tons of wheat from state reserves at disposal of SMA in Berlin.
64	Note: GOC British Troops Berlin to Military Governor CCG 215/2513	21 July	Refers to No. 63: offer is Soviet propaganda; tactics may be to ease up on on food, but rely on coal to squeeze out Western allies.
65	Tel 1629 to Berlin CCG 215/2513	23 July	Informs of press reports of Sokolovsky's demial of any blockade of Berlin and criticism of Americans.
66	Berlin tel 1459 CCG 215/2513	23 July	Refers to No. 65 and US rebuttal of Sokolovsky's allegations.
67	Washington tel 3664 CCG 215/2513	24 July	Reports statement by Clay praising courage of Berliners and announcing airlift of 4,500 tons per day.
68	Note: Military Governor to GOC British Troops Berlin CCG 215/2513	2 Aug	Attaches extract from report by manpower officer on morale of Berlin population: serious drop due to Soviet currency and shortage of food.

Four-Power Negotiations, July-September 1948

The Western allies were not initially at one on what should be their diplomatic response to the Soviet blockade of Berlin. Bevin resisted American pressure for an early approach to the Soviet Government. He told the Prime Minister, Clement Attlee, on 2 July, that Sokolovsky's letter of 29 June could not remain unanswered, and time must be allowed for a response to that letter and a meeting between Sokolovsky and the three Western Military Governors scheduled for 3 July. If nothing came of either approach, a note to the Soviet Government might be considered, but should not be presented until at least 6 July. Attlee 'entirely agreed'.[12] And when pressed by the US Ambassador in London, Lewis W Douglas, for the immediate delivery of a message to Moscow, Bevin insisted that Robertson's reply to Sokolovsky must go first. 'I should', he said, 'not be able to defend myself in the House of Commons if I had failed to explore the opening offered by Marshal Sokolovsky's letter.'[13] It was not a course which he expected to yield any positive

[12] Minute by W Strang, 2 July 1948, C 5266/3/18/G.

[13] Despatch No. 965 to Washington, 3 July 1948, C 5363/3/G.

result. A letter from Robertson to Sokolovsky of 2 July, requested information on when inter-zonal road, rail and barge traffic would be restored. But during a meeting on the following evening with Clay, Robertson and Lieutenant-General Roger Noiret, the Chief of the French Group on the Control Council, Sokolovsky simply affirmed that the situation in Berlin was directly related to the decisions taken at the London Conference. He appeared to have no authority to negotiate on the transport situation, and Clay, Noiret and Robertson were agreed 'that no further action by [themselves] in Berlin at this stage could have any useful result' (No. 69).

In London, wrangling continued over the terms of a joint note to the Soviet Government: Bevin disliked a US proposal that it should include an offer to submit the Berlin issue to the United Nations (UN), but the French would not accept the alternative of discussion by the CFM. As a result it was not until late on 5 July that a text was finally agreed.[14] Next day Bevin presented the British version of this to Georgii Zaroubin, the Soviet Ambassador in London. It asserted British rights in Berlin, insisted on the restoration of freight and passenger traffic between the Western zones and Berlin, and made the latter a prerequisite for the opening of negotiations between the four occupying authorities 'for the settlement of any question in dispute arising out of the administration of the City of Berlin' (No. 70). The Soviet reply was far from conciliatory. In a note of 14 July Zaroubin claimed that the Western Governments 'by their infringement of the agreed decisions for the government of Berlin, [had] themselves reduce[d] to nothing their right to participate in the occupation of Berlin' (No. 75). Meanwhile, although it was generally assumed in Whitehall that the Russians hoped to achieve their aims in Berlin by measures short of war, Ministers thought it 'prudent to plan on the assumption that there might be a war, as it was thought that we could not withdraw from Berlin without making the most strenuous efforts to stay there' (No. 73). It was in any case quite apparent that there was little scope for compromise on Germany in the context of a renewed meeting of the CFM, and that without four-power agreement the Russians would be likely to continue or resume their blockade of Berlin. As Sir William Strang, the Joint Permanent Under-Secretary with responsibility for the Foreign Office's German Section, pointed out in a paper of 8 July, the situation could be stressful for the Western powers and embarrassing for the Russians, 'and the question would be: Who can hold out the longest?' (No. 72).

Discussion of the Soviet note of 14 July and of how the Western allies should respond to it needs to be seen in the context of wider developments. On 19 July the Consultative Council on Western Union, established in April 1948 in accordance with the Brussels Treaty and comprising the Foreign Ministers of the five signatory powers, met at The Hague. This meeting not only provided Bevin with the opportunity to discuss the note and the Berlin situation in general with his European colleagues, but also clearly reinforced his view that the West could afford to take a tough line with the Soviet Union. As he told Sir Oliver Franks, Britain's Ambassador in Washington, on 19 July, when transmitting a draft reply to the Soviet note for discussion with the US Secretary of State, he considered it important to maintain the initiative. While remaining 'absolutely firm on our rights in Berlin', the Western powers should adopt a flexible approach in the hope of reaching a general settlement with Moscow. The Foreign Secretary considered that the Western Union meetings and parallel security talks in Washington should be a

[14] Minute by Strang, 5 July 1948, C 5382/3/18/G.

powerful deterrent to the Soviet Union. He thought they would put the West in a position 'in which [they could] contemplate resuming discussions with Soviet Union on a footing of equality if not of superiority'. In any event, Bevin felt that public opinion in Europe would not permit their proceeding to extreme measures over Berlin, involving the risk of war, without a further serious attempt at reopening conversations with the Soviet Government (No. 77).

Again, however, differences emerged between Britain and the United States over how best to deal with the Russians over Berlin. The Americans continued to favour the course that appealed least to the British: a joint and oral approach to the Soviet leader, Joseph Stalin, by the British, French and US Ambassadors in Moscow, and referral to the UN if that were to fail. As Bevin told the US Ambassador on 22 July, he was 'deeply troubled' by this proposal. The Foreign Secretary 'wished to approach the Soviet Government, not a man', and an oral approach, inviting a rebuff, was 'a weak way of doing things'. It would 'tend to build up [Stalin's] position in Europe' just when that had recently been diminished by the defiant spirit exhibited by Yugoslavia's Marshal Tito in opposition to Soviet domination of Eastern Europe (No. 80). But, as before, US policy carried the day, the resignation of the French Government on 19 July having removed the possibility of support from that quarter, and on 26 July Bevin agreed to the preparation of a short paper to be given to the Soviet Foreign Minister by the three Ambassadors in Moscow in the hope of securing an audience with Stalin. 'Our object', Bevin contended, 'should be to try to get the Russians back to the Oder. If we left Berlin now the Slavs would settle on the Rhine, and that would be the end of Western Europe' (No. 82). The allied airlift had 'powerfully affected the imagination of the people, not only of Berlin, but of the whole of Germany', and, as was reasoned in a circular telegram of 24 July, its maintenance might soon bring the Russians 'to a different state of mind' (No. 81). Indeed, Frank Roberts, Bevin's private secretary and personal representative in Moscow during the absence of the Ambassador, Sir Maurice Peterson, was 'very much struck by the affability of Stalin and [Vyacheslav] Molotov' when on 2 August he, along with the French and US Ambassadors, met the Soviet leader and his Foreign Minister (No. 86). But Stalin also proposed the drafting of a joint statement providing for the removal of all transport restrictions between Berlin and the Western zones, simultaneously with the withdrawal of Western currency from the city, and the resumption of four-power talks on Germany. He likewise made clear his desire for the suspension of the London agreements and his opposition to the establishment of a West German government (No. 85).

Bevin was not to be moved on Berlin. He rejected Molotov's claim that the Western allies had, and could have, no function whatever in connexion with the control of the Berlin currency. This, he insisted, was not a mere technical issue, but the 'very heart' of the West's differences with the Soviet Union since currency control would make the Russians the masters of the whole of Berlin. 'It is important', he wrote in a telegram to Moscow of 8 August, 'to make it plain to the Russians that we see what they are arriving at and that we are not going to put our head in the noose they are preparing for us' (No. 90). Where Soviet motives were concerned, Geoffrey Harrison, the British Minister in Moscow, thought it evident that both Stalin and Molotov had in varying degrees come to regard the division of Germany as the 'most probable development', and that this meant they would be unable to tolerate the continued sharing of authority in Berlin (No. 91). Robertson evidently felt that they had a good chance of achieving their objective. In a gloomy telegram of 10 August he warned the Foreign Office 'we cannot stay in Berlin indefinitely in defiance of the Soviet'. He doubted the ability of the Western powers to keep Berlin adequately supplied throughout the winter, and urged the need for a *modus vivendi* in order to keep the position in the city in equilibrium pending four-power discussions (No. 93). This was not a course favoured by Bevin. Nor did he incline towards the American view that if the four-power negotiations failed the situation in Berlin should be referred to the UN. 'He thinks', noted Strang, 'that we are going to pull through this crisis by sitting tight in Berlin, increasing the air lift, strengthening our position in the Western sectors, building up Western Germany, and by going on arguing stoutly with the Russians on a Four Power basis either in Moscow or in Berlin or elsewhere' (No. 96). Bevin appears, nonetheless, to have taken a more positive view than his opposite number in Washington of progress made in the Moscow negotiations towards drafting a directive for the Military Governors in Berlin on the lifting of travel restrictions, currency control and trade between Berlin and the rest of Germany (Nos. 101-04). And when subsequent discussions between the Military Governors failed to achieve agreement on these issues, Bevin successfully opposed US efforts to include in a joint communication to Moscow a reference to recent communist-led demonstrations which had paralysed the work of Berlin's City Assembly. He was, he told the US Ambassador in London, 'quite willing to make a representation to Moscow about the disorders, but not in such a way as to prevent the questions raised in the Berlin discussions from being treated on their merits' (Nos. 107 & 108).

Further talks in Moscow, in part aimed at securing some clarification of the Soviet position on Berlin, failed to resolve outstanding differences. A meeting between Molotov and Western representatives in Moscow on 14 September left Roberts under the impression that the Russians were playing for time. They, he thought, were prepared to prolong discussions indefinitely, they wanted to place the onus for any break on the West, and they intended to continue the exchanges in such a manner that it would be more difficult for the West to build up their case against them before the UN (No. 109). The Western powers responded by drafting another joint note to the Soviet Government setting out their final views on the points at issue and asking the Russians to state by 29 September whether they were prepared to remove their blockade measures and to free communications with Berlin by rail, road and water. Moreover, despite the personal doubts expressed by Roberts about the value of maintaining the West's position in Berlin, Bevin remained convinced that 'unless a firm stand were made now, our position in Europe would be hopeless'. He told the Cabinet on 22 September that 'it would be fatal to give the Soviet Government the impression that the United Kingdom would not in any circumstances oppose them by force' (Nos. 110 & 111). The documents selected below have been chosen to convey the spirit and direction of the quadripartite talks on Berlin, rather than their detail.

DOCUMENT SUMMARIES

	DOCUMENT	DATE	MAIN SUBJECT
69	Berlin tel 1287 C 5294/3/18	3 July	Reports discussion with Sokolovsky on Berlin transport

			situation: Military Governors could take no further useful action.
70	Despt 556 to Washington C 5390/3/18	6 July	Informs of delivery of note to Soviet Ambassador: HMG ready to negotiate on Berlin as soon as methods of duress lifted.
71	Berlin tel MG88 to MoD C 5483/3/18	8 July	Predicts serious difficulties in Berlin unless airlift is increased to 3,200 tons per day quickly.
72	Minute: Strang to Bevin C 5611/3/18	8 July	Attaches memo responding to Bevin's query on Berlin tel 1298: 'What should be our policy?'
73	Minutes: extract from COS(48) 96th mtg DEFE 11/321	9 July	Records discussion with Ministers of possibility of war over Berlin, and need for Western Union Command organisation.
74	Moscow tel 814 C 5521/3/18	10 July	Argues that first Soviet objective is expulsion from Berlin of Western powers, whom they think will withdraw rather than fight to stay there.
75	Tel 1399 to Moscow C 5741/3/18	14 July	Transmits text of Soviet reply to allied note on Berlin (No. 70).
76	Lübbecke tel 677 BASIC C 5745/3/18	16 July	Robertson sends Strang his personal reactions to Soviet note, which he considers 'plainly hostile': Clay's plan to send convoy up the Autobahn, he thinks, not very realistic.
77	The Hague tel 264 C 5808/3/18	19 July	Bevin instructs British Ambassador, Washington, to tell US Secretary of State that HMG favours an immediate, robust response to Soviet note.
78	The Hague tel 268 C 5811/3/18	19 July	Reports Bevin's discussion of Berlin situation with Western Union colleagues.
79	Paris tel 976 C 5898/3/18	21 July	Warns FO that French MFA think 'we should stop, look and listen before putting in another note to the Russians about Berlin'.
80	Despt 1078 to Washington C 5978/3/18	22 July	Reports that Bevin is dismayed by US views on how to approach the Soviet Government.
81	Intel 306 to selected Posts C 5873/3/18	24 July	Transmits appreciation of Berlin situation: allied ability and willingness to continue airlift may bring Russians 'to a different

			state of mind'.
82	Despt 1105 to Washington C 6207/3/18	26 July	Reports 'difficult' Anglo-American discussion on approach to Soviet Government.
83	Minutes: GEN 241/5th mtg CAB 130/38	27 July	Records ministerial discussion of proposed communication to the Soviet Government
84	Minutes: 14th mtg of Defence Committee CAB 131/5	30 July	Records discussion of defence preparations: Attlee understands COS anxieties over Berlin, but it is for Ministers to assess general political situation.
85	Moscow tel 924 C 6226/3/18	3 Aug	Reports meeting between the three Western Ambassadors and Stalin.
86	Letter: Roberts to Strang C 6546/3/18	3 Aug	Provides background information on the Moscow talks: everyone struck by 'affability' of Stalin and Molotov.
87	Tel 1578 to Moscow C 6329/3/18	4 Aug	Draft, annotated by Bevin, putting counter-arguments to Stalin's justification of blockade.
88	Moscow tel 966 C 6423/3/18	6 Aug	Reports tough meeting with Molotov: talks may be protracted.
89	MoD tel COS(W) 607 to JSM Washington MOD B/C/165	7 Aug	Instructions for an approach to US COS with a view to preliminary consideration of a meeting of Combined Chiefs of Staff in the autumn.
90	Tel 1625 to Moscow C 6423/3/18	8 Aug	Contends that allied tactics were mistaken, but: 'The battle of wills is joined and it is Molotov and not we who must give way.'
91	Moscow tel 979 C 6441/3/18	8 Aug	Analyses Soviet position and possible ways forward on Berlin.
92	Tel 8758 to Washington MOD B/C/165	9 Aug	Refers to No. 89: instructions to impress on Marshall that in the event of war with Soviet Union UK role would depend on level of US support.
93	Berlin tel 1596 C 6531/3/18	10 Aug	Expresses view: 'Our position is fundamentally weak because we cannot stay in Berlin indefinitely in defiance of the Soviet.'
94	Tel 1843 to Berlin C 6531/3/18	12 Aug	Conveys Strang's response to No. 93: need for plan for Berlin currency, which is at root of present conflict.

95	Washington tel 3897 C 6597/3/18	13 Aug	Reports difficulties in the way of holding meeting of Combined Chiefs of Staff.
96	Letter: Strang to Cadogan C 6597/3/18	13 Aug	Seeks Cadogan's advice on possible referral of Berlin question to UN.
97	Letter: Cadogan to Strang C 6884/3/18	16 Aug	Responds to No. 96: UN framework would not facilitate four-power agreement.
98	Moscow tel 1044 C 6733/3/18	17 Aug	Reports that Moscow talks had reached decisive point: time to meet Stalin.
99	Tel 1743 to Moscow C 6733/3/18	18 Aug	Reply, agreeing to No. 98: far better to be beaten in struggle to maintain position in Berlin, than to surrender on conditions.
100	Moscow tel 1091 C 6962/3/18	24 Aug	Reports on meetings with Stalin and Molotov: discussion of draft directive to Military Governors.
101	Minutes: Bevin/Attlee C 6936/3/18	24 Aug	Bevin thinks Soviet draft offers chance of reasonable settlement that should not be turned down: Prime Minister agrees.
102	Moscow tel 1108 C 7062/3/18	25 Aug	Roberts reports that Bedell Smith agrees they were 'too near agreement to justify a break'.
103	Tel 1869 to Moscow C 7086/3/18	28 Aug	Authorises Roberts to accept revised texts that cover main points insisted on by HMG.
104	Tel 2102 to Berlin C 7136/3/18	30 Aug	Conveys instructions for negotiations with Sokolovsky: Military Governors should 'work out the best solution they can'.
105	BJSM Washington tel 524 to MOD MOD B/C/165	31 Aug	US COS confirm they cannot agree to proposal for full-scale meeting of Combined Chiefs of Staff.
106	Berlin tel 1822 C 7371/3/18	8 Sept	Summarises position reached in Berlin talks: 3 outstanding points of principle, and no chance of progress until action taken on governmental level.
107	Tels 10207 & 10208 to Washington C 7442/3/18	10 Sept	Bevin thinks US attitude on joint communication to Soviet Govt could ruin chance of settlement and instructs Franks to appeal to Marshall.
108	Tel 2038 to Moscow C 7371/3/18	13 Sept	Instructions to seek early interview with Stalin to present

			joint communication on Berlin: 'this week we have a chance to get through this blockade if ever we are to do so'.
109	Moscow tel 1224 C 7583/3/18	14 Sept	Roberts reports interview with Molotov: little prospect of satisfactory agreement.
110	Letter: Roberts to Strang C 8135/3/18	14 Sept	Reflects on Soviet position on Berlin, and possibility of US acting unilaterally.
111	Cabinet Conclusions (extract) CAB 128/13	22 Sept	Bevin summarises recent developments on Berlin and receives Cabinet support for his firm policy.

Berlin at the UN, October-December 1948

By the end of September 1948, it was almost inevitable that the Berlin question would be referred to the UN Security Council (UNSC). Although Bevin remained sceptical, the failure of the Moscow and Berlin discussions combined with US pressure made it difficult to argue for any other course. The Foreign Secretary was nevertheless adamant that a definite date for the lifting of the blockade must be set before any agreement with the Soviet Government could be reached. After a further exchange of notes on 22 and 25 September, followed by the Soviet Government's publication of an account of the preceding negotiations (hitherto kept secret), the Western powers addressed a final note to the Russians on 26 September, stating their intention to refer the Berlin dispute to the UNSC as constituting a threat to international peace and security. In reply, on 3 October, the Soviet Government maintained that full responsibility for the Berlin situation lay with the Western powers, and proposed instead a meeting of the CFM. This, as Bevin made plain to the French Foreign Minister, Robert Schuman, was not a suggestion he was ready to entertain. 'M. Molotov's attitude over a period of years showed', he said, 'that Soviet policy had not changed at all since his exchanges with von Ribbentrop in 1939 and 1940. The Russians were trying to get the same things from us which they had tried to get from the Germans' (No. 112). The Americans were confident of their ability to keep Berlin supplied through the winter and, despite some misgivings on Robertson's part and a report that Truman had been considering sending the US Chief Justice, Frederick Moore Vinson, on a personal mission to Stalin, Sir Alec Cadogan, Britain's Permanent Representative to the UN, insisted that the three Western power 'were not looking for an early settlement at any price' (Nos. 114-16).

A detailed record of the events leading up to the reference of the Berlin question to the UN can be found in the White Paper published by the British Government on 11 October as Cmd. 7534 of 1948.[15] The documents in this group do not seek to duplicate that account, nor do they attempt to cover in detail the complex (and tedious) discussions that followed the opening of the Berlin debate in the UNSC, then sitting in Paris, on 4 October. The Soviet Government denied the Council's competence to discuss Berlin, but the six 'disinterested' members, led by the Council Chairman, the Argentine Foreign Minister, Juan Bramuglia, attempted to

[15] See note 9 above.

find a compromise, and on 25 October a resolution calling for the simultaneous lifting of the Berlin blockade and the summoning of a meeting of the four Military Governors to arrange for the introduction of the Soviet zone mark as the sole currency in Berlin received nine affirmative votes. This, however, was vetoed by the Soviet Union, and a joint appeal made on 13 November by Trygve Lie, the UN Secretary-General, and Herbert Evatt, the Australian Minister for External Affairs and President of the UN General Assembly (UNGA), for the opening of four-power talks was rejected by the three Western powers on the grounds that such talks must be preceded by the lifting of the blockade. Bramuglia continued to meet with the delegations of the four occupying powers, concentrating upon the technical problem of 'simultaneity' between the lifting of the blockade and the introduction of the Soviet zone currency, and on 1 December a Committee of Experts representing the six disinterested UNSC powers was established to prepare recommendations on these issues. The Americans were nonetheless very doubtful about what the experts could achieve. They questioned the relevance of the Committee's preliminary currency report to a Berlin whose administration was already effectively divided, and by the end of the year Bevin was at odds with them over their desire for the early introduction of the Deutsche Mark as the sole currency of the Western sectors. Bevin feared that since it was the Western powers who had taken the Berlin dispute to the UNSC, they 'would be placing themselves in a very weak position and would be very vulnerable to Soviet propaganda if they were now to refuse to consider on its technical merits the plan produced by the Experts' (No. 134).

During the last quarter of 1948 Berlin was eclipsed as an issue of pressing international concern by other problems, in particular that of Palestine. The UN sought in vain to impose its authority following the assassination by Zionists of its mediator, Count Bernadotte, on 17 September, three days before his report was submitted to the General Assembly proposing that hostilities should be brought to an end on the basis that 'a Jewish state called Israel exists in Palestine and that there are no sound reasons for assuming that it will not continue to do so'.[16] Both Palestine and the Berlin blockade were brought into the political debate between the candidates for the US presidential election on 2 November which resulted in Truman's somewhat unexpected victory. In the case of Berlin, the debate tended to dissipate and confuse the focus of official US policy. At the same time other German issues, including the establishment of an international authority for the Ruhr and proposals for changing the German reparations programme, involved the British Government in a delicate balancing act between the US and France. In Cabinet discussion on 22 December 1948, the question was posed: 'Should we regard [Western Germany] as a potential ally against Soviet aggression, or should our predominant concern be to render it impossible for her to become once again a menace to world peace or a military asset in hostile hands?'[17] Although, as Bevin pointed out, it was premature to reach any firm conclusions about Germany's long-term policy, this question underlay discussion of the Berlin situation at governmental level.

DOCUMENT SUMMARIES

[16] Cmd. 7530, *Progress Report of the United Nations Mediator on Palestine* (London: HMSO, 16 September 1948), p. 35.

[17] CM(48)82nd Conclusions.

	DOCUMENT	DATE	MAIN SUBJECT
112	Extract from record of Anglo-French meeting C 8260/3/18	2 Oct	Bevin emphasises need for extreme care in dealing with the Russians, based on past experience.
113	Extract from record of tripartite meeting C 8613/3/18	4 Oct	Marshall considered allies were 'buying time' in Berlin, and were in a stronger position than they realised.
114	Berlin tel 1978 C 8205/3/18	6 Oct	Robertson suggests to Kirkpatrick attempt to reach agreement with the Soviet Union in parallel with UN: FO minute doubts wisdom of this plan.
115	Tel 2414 to Berlin C 8205/3/18	7 Oct	Kirkpatrick reports that Bevin agrees with first 3 paras of No. 114, but cannot go back on his agreement to work through UNSC.
116	Paris tel 1443 C 8408/3/18	12 Oct	Cadogan describes talks with Gen. McNaughton who passed on information about progress of Bramuglia and the Six.
117	Paris tel 1444 C 8409/3/18	12 Oct	From Cadogan, commenting on No. 116 and speculating on Soviet response.
118	Paris tel 1457 C 8446/3/18	14 Oct	Reports tripartite meeting on Berlin: French view of tactics differs from that of US and UK.
119	Minute: Kirkpatrick to Bevin C 8953/3/18	21 Oct	French Ambassador says his Government will not agree to any currency move in Berlin while matter is before UNSC.
120	Memo by Dean with minutes C 8874/3/18	26 Oct	Sets out next steps in Berlin situation, including pros and cons of referral to UNGA.
121	Record of FO meeting C 9126/3/18	7 Nov	Bevin asks that plan for Berlin currency be prepared ready to be put forward to UNSC if required.
122	FO memos C 10106/3/18	20 & 23 Nov	Embody replies of British, French, Soviet and US Govts to questions put by UNSC President to the occupying powers.
123	UKDEL Paris tel 607 C 9813/3/18	30 Nov	Reports UNSC President's decision to appoint committee to work on trade and financial arrangements for Berlin.
124	Minute by Serpell on letter from Robertson to	30 Nov	Comments on Robertson's statement that if no move is

No.	Document	Date	Summary
	Strang T 236/2011		made on Berlin currency before elections it will be too late.
125	UKDEL Paris tel 679 C 9978/3/18	5 Dec	From Minister of State, reporting message from Marshall, who was anxious that early decision on Berlin currency be made at governmental level.
126	Tel 794 to UKDEL Paris C 9978/3/18	6 Dec	Reply to No. 125: question was to be put to Cabinet and could not be rushed.
127	Tel 2782 to Berlin C 9978/3/18	7 Dec	Asks Robertson what further steps Russians might take if Western currency was introduced throughout Western sectors of Berlin.
128	Berlin tel 2273 C 10112/3/18	8 Dec	Reply to No. 127: measures include sealing off Western sectors, disrupting electricity supplies, cutting cable communications and S-Bahn.
129	Cabinet Conclusions (extract) CAB 128/13	9 Dec	Cabinet agrees Bevin should seek agreement with US and France on plan for introducing Western mark as sole currency in western sectors; no announcement till UNSC Committee of Experts reports.
130	Tel 3790 to Paris C 10093/3/18	10 Dec	Informs UKDEL Paris that Robertson has been instructed to consult secretly with US and French colleagues on currency scheme for Western sectors.
131	UKDEL Paris tel 772 C 10206/3/18	11 Dec	Cadogan reports currency committee has met Western experts and hopes to report on 22-23 Dec.
132	Tel 3841 to Paris C 10206/3/18	14 Dec	Comments on No. 131: important to maintain engagement with committee to prevent it adopting an 'unrealistic or undesirable' plan.
133	Note: Strang to Bevin C 10535/3/18	17 Dec	Records views of US Ambassador on work of Committee of Experts and advises against interference: Bevin minutes agreement.
134	Tel 13712 to Washington C 10608/3/18	31 Dec	Bevin disagrees with State Dept views on how to proceed with Committee of Experts' report, which must be considered on its merits.

The Lifting of the Blockade, February-May 1949

Intergovernmental wrangling over the Committee of Experts' plan for the adoption under four-power control of the Soviet zone mark as the sole currency of Berlin continued into January 1949. The three Western powers were united in their opposition to any project which might result in the Soviet domination of the economy of their sectors. But while British and French experts were, along with their Soviet counterpart, ready to accept the Committee's plan as a basis for discussion, the US expert regarded it as 'completely unacceptable' and produced counter-proposals he considered more appropriate to an administratively divided Berlin. The danger, as Bevin appreciated, was that transatlantic differences would be exposed and the Committee of Experts would eventually lay most of the blame for its failure to work out a satisfactory plan on the attitude of the Western powers. This, however, was essentially a tactical problem which had to be set alongside the success of the airlift during the winter of 1948-49 and progress made in rejuvenating the West German economy. Bevin was certainly in no mood to surrender the political gains he felt the West had secured as a result of its standing firm on Berlin. Indeed, on 31 January 1949 Stalin, in reply to a question from an American journalist, Joseph Kingsbury Smith, indicated his readiness to lift the blockade if the Western powers agreed to postpone the establishment of a West German state, pending a meeting of the CFM. Stalin, significantly, made no mention of the currency issue. Nonetheless, in a Cabinet memorandum of 4 February Bevin argued that Britain should 'resolve not to conclude any agreement with the Soviet Government which would involve postponing or checking either the creation of a Western German Government or the incorporation of Western Germany in our Western system' (No. 135).

The Americans meanwhile seemed ready to assume a more conciliatory approach. Dean Acheson, Marshall's successor as US Secretary of State, instructed Philip Jessup, the US Deputy Representative to the UNSC, to sound out Yakov Malik, the Soviet UN Representative, on Stalin's intentions, and in March informal discussions began on the lifting of the Soviet blockade.[18] Bevin learnt of these talks when early in April he and Schuman visited Washington for the signing of the North Atlantic Treaty. He remained, however, cautious about the notion of linking the lifting of the blockade to an early meeting of the CFM. He thought it essential to consolidate the situation in Western Europe before going any further with the Russians. 'If they were really prepared to end the blockade', he told Acheson, '... we should insist on discussing not only Berlin and Germany, but Austria, Trieste, Greece, our rights in the Balkan satellite countries and indeed Europe as a whole' (No. 139). Attlee, agreed: the allies, he thought, should press on with the establishment of Western European programmes and a West German government. 'We should then', Attlee concluded, 'be in a much stronger position to discuss with the Russians the whole German problem ... and in a better position to ensure that any agreement which might be reached with the Russians would not immediately be employed by them to gain control over the whole of Germany' (No. 140). Schuman, by contrast, was much more sympathetic to American proposals for a communication to the Soviet Government setting out a timetable for the ending of the blockade and a CFM meeting in early June, prior to the formation of a West German government (No. 143). And Bevin was evidently disturbed by such comments as that by George Kennan, Chief of the State Department's Policy

[18] *FRUS 1949*, vol. iii, pp. 694-751.

Planning Staff, that the Department was worried about how far the US delegation at the CFM 'should go in supporting the formation of a unified Germany' (No. 152). The remark, made on 28 April to Sir Frederick Hoyer Millar, the British Minister in Washington, seemed to suggest that the Americans were inclining towards compromise.

Bevin expressed his disquiet to Acheson in a personal message of 29 April. In this he emphasised that four-power negotiations on Germany would not be easy, that Soviet 'ideas and objects [were] exactly opposed to ours', and that the Russians were thinking in terms of a 'heavily centralised totalitarian State, controlled by the Communists by direct or indirect methods, geared to the economy of the Eastern European States and the Soviet Union and bitterly hostile to Western Europe and America'. They would, he thought, try to use a CFM meeting to foster public opposition, especially in France, to the ratification of the North Atlantic Treaty. 'I fear', he added, there is too much readiness in some quarters to believe that merely because the Russians have shown some readiness to raise the blockade the rest will be plain-sailing' (No. 154). With this Acheson expressed his full agreement. But he still thought the projected four-power meeting worthwhile as a propaganda exercise, especially if the Western powers were able to come forward with 'some pretty large and constructive proposals' (No. 157). In any event, by 4 May Britain, France, the Soviet Union and the United States had managed to agree on the lifting of all restrictions imposed since 1 March 1948 on communications, transport and trade across sector and zone borders on 12 May 1949 and the convening of a meeting of the CFM in Paris on 23 May. The news was celebrated in Berlin with public demonstrations and speechmaking (No. 161). Bevin was nevertheless of the opinion that the Russians were far from calling off their cold war in Germany. Western governments, he cautioned the British Ambassador in Washington, 'would do well to keep continually in mind that after losing an important battle, but only a battle, in Germany, Russia is now suing for an armistice in order to gain time, though not yet for peace' (No. 158).

DOCUMENT SUMMARIES

	DOCUMENT	DATE	MAIN SUBJECT
135	Memo by Bevin GEN 241/4, CAB 130/38	**1949** 4 Feb	Summarises position on Berlin and West German political programme; recommends holding firm, continuing airlift and going ahead with establishment of West German government.
136	GEN 241/9th mtg CAB 130/38	7 Feb	Ministers endorse Bevin's policy proposals in No. 135.
137	Berlin tel 337 C 2099/15/18	10 Mar	Refers to No. 128 and reviews additional steps Russians might take in Berlin, and possible counter-measures.
138	UKDEL New York tel 634 C 2417/14/18	21 Mar	Information from Jessup on his conversations with Soviet Ambassador: opening of exchanges on Berlin.

139	Washington tel 1854 C 2765/23/18	1 Apr	From Bevin for Strang: discussion with Acheson of Jessup-Malik talks; Bevin wants Western European issues settled before negotiating on Berlin.
140	Tel 3638 to Washington C 2765/23/18	1 Apr	From Attlee for Bevin, approving his cautious attitude in No. 139: 'this is not the moment to put ourselves in the position of making requests to the Russians.'
141	GEN 241/10th mtg CAB 130/38	4 Apr	Refers to Nos. 139-40: Ministers agree not to oppose idea of CFM as price for lifting of Berlin blockade, provided establishment of West German government is safeguarded first.
142	Minutes: Kirkpatrick to Attlee and Bevin C 3167/23/18	14 Apr	Sets out tentative programme for agreement on Berlin and meeting of CFM, to be discussed with Bevin on his return.
143	Paris tel 430 C 3267/23/18	20 Apr	Harvey reports that Schuman favours US timetable for note to Soviet Government on ending of blockade and meeting of CFM.
144	Tel 1164 to Paris C 3267/23/18	20 Apr	Reply to No. 143: Bevin is convinced time is not yet right for approach to Russians.
145	Tel 1524 to UKDEL New York C 3166/23/18	20 Apr	Recapitulates for Cadogan history of exchanges with Russians over Berlin: latter must not be allowed to prevent formation of West German government.
146	Tel 4581 to Washington C 3413/23/18	26 Apr	Expresses concern at statement on Jessup-Malik talks by State Dept, who should be asked to issue revised version.
147	Washington tel 2366 C 3533/23/18	26 Apr	Transmits redrafted text of State Dept's oral communication to be made to Russians.
148	Tel 4601 to Washington C 3533/23/18	27 Apr	Instructs Ambassador to thank Acheson for amending draft communication to Russians.
149	UKDEL New York tel 1041 C 3554/23/18	27 Apr	Comments on Jessup's meeting with Malik, reported in No. 150.
150	UKDEL New York tel 1042 C 3555/23/18	27 Apr	Transmits Jessup's record of meeting with Malik, who would now seek Vyshinsky's approval that agreement has been reached on Berlin.
151	Tel 1535 BASIC to Frankfurt/Main	28 Apr	Refers to Nos. 149-50 and asks Robertson's views urgently on

	C 3555/23/18		detail of lifting of Berlin restrictions and currency issues.
152	Washington tel 2413 C 3606/23/18	28 Apr	Reports conversation between Hoyer Millar and Kennan: State Dept were worried about Soviet intentions, and how far CFM should go in supporting formation of a united Germany.
153	Frankfurt/Main tel 779 BASIC C 3615/23/18	28 Apr	Reply to No. 152, with minutes by Dean and Seal who agree with Robertson's judgement on what is important to secure in Berlin agreement.
154	Tel 4671 to Washington C 3687/23/18	28 Apr	Instructs Franks to deliver personal message to Acheson expressing Bevin's disquiet at implications of proposed CFM discussions.
155	Tel 1720 to UKDEL New York C 3554/23/18	29 Apr	Instructions for Cadogan in the light of Nos. 149-50 and 153, to be discussed with Jessup and Chauvel.
156	Berlin tel 560 C 3706/23/18	2 May	Robertson reports conversation with Clay who thinks Soviets have 'capitulated entirely'; if so, detailed agreement on Berlin not necessary.
157	Washington tel 2467 C 3799/23/18	2 May	From Franks to Bevin: message in No. 154 had been delivered to Acheson, who agreed: 'everything depended upon maintaining the common front'.
158	Tel 4777 to Washington C 3606/23/18	2 May	Refers to No. 152: agrees with Kennan; like US, UK is committed to German unification but only if democratic government safeguarded.
159	Berlin tel 1538 BASIC C 4474/23/18	3 May	Robertson reports on German affairs: 'there is now general expectation that the blockade will shortly be raised'.
160	UKDEL New York tel 1130 C 3793/23/18	4 May	Transmits text of communiqué agreed by four powers: Berlin restrictions to be lifted on 12 May, with CFM meeting on 23 May in Paris.
161	Berlin tel 625 C 4085/23/18	13 May	Reports meetings held in Berlin on 12 May to celebrate lifting of blockade.

The Berlin Population and the Airlift, August 1948-May 1949

The position of the Western allies in Berlin was, as documents in this group indicate, to a large extent dependent upon the morale of the citizens of the beleaguered city. That in turn could not be divorced from the success or failure of the airlift in maintaining the supply of food and fuel to the Western sectors. Yet the confidence frequently exhibited by the Americans in the ability of the Western powers to sustain this operation was not always shared by their British allies. Robertson for one doubted whether the airlift could provide a permanent answer to the blockade. In a minute of 23 September 1948 he noted that it 'must fail in the end', and that the morale of the people would 'fail eventually'. He thought that for the Western allies to plan to stay on in Berlin indefinitely was 'not sensible', and that 'on no account must [they] hang on until the last possible moment and then withdraw in precipitate disorder' (No. 165). Robertson was, however, far from being a defeatist on the wider issue of Germany and relations with the Soviet Union. He had been impressed by the courage and determination shown by the Germans when faced by the blockade. Moreover, as he made clear in a letter to Strang of 30 September, he believed the West to be 'committed to war with the Russians eventually', that Berlin was the 'epitome of the German situation as a whole', and that the time had come to 'give to the Germans psychological support on a scale altogether different from that they [were] receiving from [the West] at the present time' (No. 168).

Robertson was confirmed in his estimate of the German readiness to resist Soviet pressure by the elections held in the Western sectors on 5 December 1948 for a new City Assembly. Since the beginning of the crisis the Soviet Union had continued to exploit inter-allied differences, and had introduced measures to widen the East-West split in the administration of Berlin. The democratic majority of the City Assembly and most of the administration which had previously functioned from the City Hall in the Soviet sector were forced to transfer their headquarters to the Western sectors, and on 30 November the SED and other communist-controlled groups established in the Opera House what was in effect a Soviet puppet *Magistrat.* Five days later the Social Democrats gained 64.5% of the votes in the municipal elections in the West and set about trying to build a united anti-communist front with the Christian Democratic Union (CDU) and the Liberal Democrats. In Robertson's view the new administration, and Reuter, now *Regierender Bürgermeister* (Governing Mayor) of West Berlin, would improve the conduct of affairs generally, providing ordered government free from Soviet interference. The Western sectors were, however, almost a 'homogeneous Western island in a Soviet sea'. They remained difficult to supply and, Robertson predicted, would be compelled to accept further economy measures such as the virtual cessation of industry, the reduction of transport and harsher conditions in hospitals and schools (No. 173).

By January 1949, Robertson was still able to report that morale remained high and that there was no inclination to abandon the struggle. The winter had been unexpectedly mild and conditions were better than expected. The steady increase in the airlift also gave encouragement and on 18 February the millionth ton was flown into Berlin. Employment had been maintained at a higher level than expected and the Russians and the German communists had not reacted violently to the elections. And if few people saw clearly any final solution of the Berlin problem, there was a general belief that if the Western allies remained firm, intensified the counter-blockade and steadily improved conditions in the Western sectors by means of the airlift, the Russians would sooner or later be compelled to give way (Nos. 177-79). Even at the end of April, when the Jessup-Malik conversations were nearing their conclusion, Bevin continued to insist on the need to maintain the airlift until the conclusion of the proposed CFM meeting. He thought it necessary to supplement the building up of stocks, to maintain morale, and to ensure that the airlift could be resumed if alternative arrangements for supplying the city broke down. He was prepared, as soon as the lifting of the blockade had taken effect and the way was clear for the four-power meeting, to reduce the rate of the lift, but he thought this a good opportunity to give the crews some leave, while maintaining the organisation (No. 182). It was not until the middle of July that Bevin would tell Cabinet that the British and United States Military Governors in Germany advised that, in view of the accumulation of stocks, the airlift could now be discontinued. However, the Foreign Secretary contended that Russia's future policy in Germany was uncertain; and matters should be so arranged that it would be possible to build up the airlift again to its full scale within a period of ninety days (No. 184).

DOCUMENT SUMMARIES

	DOCUMENT	DATE	MAIN SUBJECT
162	Minute: Stevens to Bevin CO 520/131/1	**1948** 3 Aug	Summarises MoD estimate on capabilities of the airlift, with draft letter to Robertson: neither UK nor US would modify their policy.
163	Despt 1145 to Washington C 6558/3/18	10 Aug	Records conversation between US Ambassador and Bevin, who urged 'resolute and determined action to resist the Russian efforts to drive us out of Berlin.'
164	Minute: Hudson to Bevin CO 520/129	10 Sept	Proposals from Minister for Air for chartering aircraft.
165	Minute: Robertson to Strang CCG 215/2547	23 Sept	Comments on Berlin situation, and need to avoid precipitate withdrawal or war: 'we should get out first and go to war afterwards.'
166	Tel 2177 BASIC to Berlin T 236/1025	24 Sept	Seeks Governor's advice on British contribution to airlift throughout the winter.
167	Frankfurt/Main tel 666 BASIC T 236/1025	30 Sept	Responds to No. 166, giving airlift figures necessary to meet minimum requirements in Western sectors.
168	Letter: Robertson to Strang C 9101/71/18	30 Sept	Considers implications of airlift for Berlin and West Germany: recommends 're-orientation of mind' towards the Germans.
169	Memo by German Section, Supply Dept	4 Oct	Reviews airlift in the light of one hundred days' experience.

	CO 520/131/1		
170	Letter: Kirkpatrick to Robertson C 9101/71/18	14 Oct	Comments on No. 168, particularly on Whitehall attitudes to Germany.
171	Berlin tel 2047 C 8628/3/18	20 Oct	Reports tightening of controls over traffic from Soviet zone to Western sectors.
172	Minute: Kinnear to Givan C 8936/3/18	21 Oct	Seeks Treasury approval to charter aircraft in order to reach minimum tonnage of 1,120 per day.
173	Berlin tel 2274 C 10113/3/18	8 Dec	Robertson summarises situation in Berlin after municipal elections.
174	Minute: Stevens to Bevin CO 520/154	31 Dec	Comments on attached letter from Robertson: only way to increase airlift was greater use by C54s of airfields in British zone.
175	Tel 87 to Berlin C 632/14/18	**1949** 18 Jan	Asks Robertson's views on airlift requirements before taking decision on Experts' currency report.
176	Berlin tel 114 C 699/14/18	24 Jan	Reply to No. 175: detailed answer not yet ready, but airlift now working with 'greatly increased efficiency and smoothness'.
177	Berlin tel 115 C 700/14/18	24 Jan	Appreciation of state of public morale in Western sectors.
178	Minute: Kirkpatrick to Bevin covering tel 1961 to Berlin CO 520/154	17 Feb	Suggests congratulatory message on delivery of millionth ton of supplies: Bevin agrees, and message sent to Robertson.
179	Reports by German Section, Finance Dept CO 707/349	19 Feb	Information bulletins compiled after six months of the Berlin airlift.
180	Memo by Research Dept C 2278/30/18	28 Feb	Examines attitude of population in the Soviet zone: clandestine activities.
181	Memo by German Section, Supply Dept CO 707/339	22 Apr	Report on food situation in Berlin after nine months of the airlift.
182	Tel 4656 to Washington C 3637/23/18	29 Apr	Refers to Jessup-Malik talks: Bevin considers it essential to maintain airlift at least until CFM concludes.
183	Berlin despt 55 C 4558/14/18	19 May	Robertson's report on Bevin's visit to Berlin and the British zone of Germany, 7-9 May.

184	Cabinet Conclusions (extract) CAB 128/16	18 July	Cabinet agrees proposals to discontinue the Berlin airlift.

CHAPTER II
Berlin Divided
1959-1961

By the time of the lifting of the Berlin blockade the division of Germany and its capital seemed well on its way to becoming permanent. The blockade, whilst exacerbating existing differences amongst the occupying powers, hastened moves towards the establishment on 23 May 1949 of the Federal Republic of Germany (FRG) within the three Western zones of occupation. Five months later, on 7 October, the functions of the Soviet military administration in Eastern Germany were assumed by a newly-proclaimed German Democratic Republic (GDR) which declared East Berlin its capital and seat of government. But Britain, France and the United States were anxious to maintain their rights in Greater Berlin and, like the Soviet Union, they were reluctant to sanction any move which might challenge the fiction of quadripartite control. Thus, while the city was represented in the upper and lower houses of the West German parliament, they opposed their sectors' acquiring the status of a separate constituent *Land* of the Federal Republic. The FRG remained in any case subject to the post-war Statute of Occupation, though progress was soon made towards the lifting of restrictions on its economic and external relations. Moreover, its participation in bodies aimed at fostering Western European integration and interdependence, such as the Council of Europe and the Coal and Steel Community, and in negotiations for the creation of a European Defence Community, signalled its emergence as an independent actor on the international stage. Stalin's proposal in the spring of 1952 for the neutralisation of a reunited Germany failed to halt this process, and with the foundation of a West German defence force, the *Bundeswehr*, and the FRG's entry into the North Atlantic Treaty Organisation (NATO) in May 1955, the Occupation Statute lapsed. Meanwhile, in the wake of a popular rising in June 1953 against the East German régime, less repressive economic measures were introduced in the East, the Soviet Government relaxed its demand for reparations, and in May 1955 the GDR was included as a charter member of the Warsaw Pact, the alliance linking the Soviet Union to its European satellites. An East German National People's Army, a professional military force at whose core were the already existing People's Police units, came officially into being in March 1956.

A War of Attrition, April-December 1959

A democratic, liberal and increasingly prosperous West German state exercised a powerful magnetic pull upon the citizens of an East Germany, which was democratic in name only and whose economic performance rarely matched that of its neighbour. One result was a steady flow of migrants from East to West, most of whom took advantage of the still open borders in Berlin. In the first fortnight of August 1953 20,000 East Germans crossed into West Berlin, and in 1960 probably in excess of 200,000 moved westwards. Their loss was a costly drain upon the GDR's economy, and during the late 1950s the SED leadership and its patrons in Moscow concentrated increasingly upon Berlin as the key to resolving the problem. Evidently anxious to strengthen the GDR, Nikita Khrushchev, the General Secretary of the Soviet Communist Party, declared on 10 November 1958 in a public address in the Sports Palace in Moscow, that the military occupation of Berlin must come to an end and that the Soviet Union intended to hand over to the GDR those functions that it presently exercised there. The Western powers should, he added, establish their own relations with the GDR if they were interested in questions connected with Berlin.[1] Then, on 27 November, in notes delivered to British, French and United States Ambassadors in Moscow, the Soviet Government accused their governments of violating the main provisions of the Potsdam Agreement and of using their position in Berlin to pursue subversive activities against the Soviet bloc. In order to put an end to 'the abnormal and dangerous situation', Khrushchev proposed that West Berlin should be made a 'demilitarised free city'. The notes were, in effect, an ultimatum, since they specified a period of six months for negotiating the change in the position of Berlin, during which time the arrangements for the communications of the three Western powers between Berlin and the FRG would be left unchanged. If this period were not used 'for achieving the appropriate agreement', the USSR threatened to execute the measures indicated by agreement with the East German régime, which, it maintained, 'like any other independent State should ... exercise its sovereignty on land, water and in the air'. If the Western powers refused to accept the 'free city' proposal, the Soviet Government would consider that there remained 'no subject for talks between the former occupying Powers on the Berlin question'.[2] Further Soviet notes followed on 13 December 1958 and 10 January 1959, the latter containing annexed copies of a draft peace treaty with Germany which foresaw the creation of a federation of two German states and a free-city solution for Berlin.[3]

The three Western occupying powers and the FRG replied on 16 February 1959 to the Soviet proposals, suggesting the holding of a four-power conference, to which German advisers should be invited, to deal with all aspects of the German problem. The British reply reaffirmed the Western powers' reservation of 'the right to uphold by all appropriate means their communications with their sectors of Berlin'. It also stated the British Government's readiness to participate in a four-power conference of Foreign Ministers, the date and place of which should be fixed by mutual agreement, through diplomatic channels.[4] Both Harold Macmillan, the Prime Minister, and Selwyn Lloyd, the Foreign Secretary, had the opportunity to discuss Berlin and the broader German question with the Soviet leadership when they visited Moscow from 21 February until 3 March. They were there able to agree with the Russians on the need for early negotiations between interested governments with a view to establishing a basis for the resolution of differences.[5] And although Krushchev continued to insist on Western acceptance of the independence of the GDR within its existing frontiers,[6] in a speech at Leipzig on 5 March he announced that the deadline of 27 March, which had previously been fixed by the Soviet Government for a settlement, could be extended 'at least until 27th June', or even to July. Four days later, he further explained in Berlin that

[1] Cmnd. 1552, *Selected Documents on Germany and the Question of Berlin, 1944-1961* (London: HMSO, 1961), pp. 314-18.

[2] *Ibid.*, pp. 318-33.

[3] *Ibid.*, pp. 351-69. Central Office of Information, *Berlin and the Problem of German Unification* (London, 1969), pp., 22-23.

[4] Cmnd. 670, *Documents about the future of Germany (including Berlin), January to February 1959* (London: HMSO, 1959), p. 19. See *FRUS 1958-1960*, vol. viii, pp. 371-72.

[5] Cmnd. 689, *Anglo-Soviet Communiqué on the discussions of the Prime Miniser of the United Kingdom, Mr. Harold Macmillan, and the Foreign Secretary, Mr. Selwyn Lloyd, with the Chairman of the Council of Ministers of the Union of the Soviet Socialist Republics, Mr. N.S. Khrushchev*, Moscow, 21 Feb 1959 (London: HMSO, 1959), p. 2.

[6] Moscow telegrams Nos. 373 and 422 of 26 February and 3 March 1959, PREM 11/2715-6.

Western and neutral forces might be stationed in West Berlin to safeguard its status as a 'Free City', though he made it plain that he considered Berlin the capital of the GDR.[7]

The British, French and US Governments meanwhile responded positively to a proposal from Khrushchev for a meeting of Foreign Ministers. In notes delivered in Moscow on 26 March they proposed that a four-power conference of Foreign Ministers should assemble in Geneva on 11 May; that the agenda 'should be questions relating to Germany, including a peace treaty with Germany and the question of Berlin'; and its purpose should be 'to reach positive agreement over as wide a field as possible', narrowing the differences between the respective points of view, and 'to prepare constructive proposals for consideration by a conference of Heads of Government later in the summer'. The projected summit could then 'consider and, if possible, resolve some wider problems' as previously referred to it and, where necessary, 'establish machinery for further negotiation'. The 'legitimate and direct interest' of Poland and Czechoslovakia and other countries 'in certain matters which would come under discussion' was also recognised, and the possibility of their participation at a certain stage of the negotiations contemplated. On 30 March the Soviet Government agreed. But within barely a fortnight of its convening the Geneva Conference was in what Selwyn Lloyd described as 'rather an exasperating state'. The danger of war receded. The Russians, nonetheless, continued to insist that, while they were prepared to give guarantees regarding Berlin's freedom and access to it, the occupation status of must be ended; and the Western powers maintained, that though they were ready to agree to a ceiling for their troop numbers in Berlin, there could be no change in the city's status pending German reunification (No. 186).

Senior officials in Whitehall were also aware that the West's stance on Berlin was not legally unassailable, particularly as the establishment of the Federal Republic had in effect brought an end to the post-war occupation régime. Philip de Zulueta, Macmillan's Private Secretary, considered the only value of the maintenance of the present theoretical basis for the status of West Berlin was that it put the Russians on notice that the Western powers regarded their half of the city as an area they would 'defend by force if necessary'. Indeed, in a paper which seemed to anticipate the détente diplomacy of the following decade, de Zulueta suggested that the Russians might be persuaded to relax their hold gradually on Eastern Europe if they felt secure, and that the West should 'encourage them by pretending to look the other way' (No. 188). Macmillan was for his part anxious to know exactly where matters would stand in the event of the Soviet Union signing a peace treaty with the GDR and the latter moving to impose 'unacceptable conditions' on traffic between Berlin and the FRG. He had lately been reading a good deal about the uncertainties arising from Britain's role during the war crisis of 1914 and, he explained to Selwyn Lloyd, he wished to be 'quite certain' that HMG was in 'no danger of drifting into something very similar over the various military and diplomatic "contingency plans" about Berlin' (No. 189). This view the Prime Minister reiterated at a meeting of the Defence Committee on 18 September, and John Killick, Assistant Head of the Foreign Office's Western Department, subsequently drafted a paper designed to provide a comprehensive picture of what might be involved in the event of such a crisis (No. 193). Yet, long before then, interest in the proceedings at Geneva had

[7] Assessment of Krushchev's visit to GDR by Maj-Gen F D Rome (Berlin), 18 March 1958, WG 1015/195.

dwindled, and on 5 August the Conference adjourned. The Russians appear to have recognised that they were unlikely to secure anything more from it than an interim agreement, which would allow the Western powers to claim that their rights in Berlin remained unaffected. Moreover, a visit by the US Vice-President, Richard Nixon, to the Soviet Union in late July, and Khrushchev's acceptance of an invitation to the United States, raised the prospect of more progress being made in bilateral discussions between the superpowers.

There were hopes in the West that a period of improved relations with the Soviet Union would now follow. The communiqué issued after private talks between the US President, Dwight D Eisenhower, and Krushchev at Camp David on 27 September said that an understanding on Berlin had been reached. Subject to the approval of the other parties directly concerned, the communiqué went on to state that negotiations would be reopened with a view to achieving a solution.[8] At a press conference in Washington on 28 September, Eisenhower said that he and the Soviet leader 'agreed ... that these negotiations [on the Berlin question] should not be prolonged indefinitely but there would be no fixed limit on them'.[9] Khrushchev subsequently confirmed this. Reaction to these developments in West Berlin itself was mixed. Its citizens were relieved that the Soviet time limit had disappeared, but feared that Khrushchev might have led Eisenhower 'a few steps up the garden path'. They were, according to a report from one British diplomat, worried lest the Americans were seriously contemplating a deal with the Russians, which would be made to some extent at Berlin's expense (No. 192). Nevertheless, in London Macmillan was encouraged to think in terms of a summit meeting with the American, French and Soviet leaders at which Berlin would undoubtedly be discussed. 'The tangible prospect of further international meetings and visits', he observed, 'should discourage hasty and violent action' (No. 195). Sir Patrick Reilly, the British Ambassador in Moscow, was similarly of the opinion that Khrushchev was now committed to a policy of détente, though he argued that the Soviet leader still needed an agreement on Berlin, and that this could only be presented as a success if it could be 'portrayed to the Soviet and East German public as at best a preliminary to the disappearance of the "occupation regime"'. It would be up to the Western powers to insist on a fairly high price for it, particularly with regard to its duration and the level of troops in Berlin (No. 197).

DOCUMENT SUMMARIES

	DOCUMENT	DATE	MAIN SUBJECT
185	Letter: Ledwidge to Wilkinson WG 1015/195	**1959** 6 April	Reviews the Berlin situation as seen from East and West: some relaxation of tension.
186	Geneva tel 132 Codel WG 1015/264	1 June	Lloyd reports to Macmillan on stalemate reached at Geneva.
187	Tel 373 Codel to Geneva WG 1015/287	9 June	Macmillan replies to Lloyd: 'the world is not interested in what we say our rights are but rather in whether in fact

[8] *FRUS 1958-1960*, vol. ix, p. 50.

[9] Washington telegram No. 2068 of 29 September 1959, WG 1015/361.

			we are able to exercise them'.
188	Minute: de Zulueta to Macmillan PREM 11/2718	18 June	Submits papers (not reproduced) setting out minimum British requirements on Berlin.
189	Minute: Macmillan to Lloyd CAB 21/3211	26 June	Asks for report on 'where we stand' on Berlin: must not drift into war as in 1914.
190	Exchange of minutes: Ledwidge/Drinkall/ Hancock WG 1015/357	27 July	Discuss Soviet tactics on Berlin and possibility of Russians agreeing to West Berlin becoming a *Land* of the FRG.
191	Minute: Rumbold to Dean WG 1015/352	18 Aug	Covers draft brief on Berlin and Germany for PM's use before he sees US President.
192	Letter: Ledwidge to Wilkinson WG 1015/363	30 Sept	Notes disquiet in West Berlin that Khrushchev may have led Eisenhower 'up the garden path'.
193	Minute by Killick CAB 21/3211	8 Oct	Covers draft outline of British position on Berlin contingency planning.
194	Minute: Tomkins to Lloyd WG 1623/75	29 Oct	Indicates problem likely to arise over flying of East German flags on the *S-Bahn*.
195	CRO tel 1060 to Canberra PREM 11/2712	10 Nov	Personal message from Macmillan to Menzies: he favoured a summit, but was happy for US to make the running in view of French and German sensitivities.
196	Minute by Drinkall WG 1015/337	25 Nov	Discusses significance of *Tass* statement on Western rights in Berlin.
197	Moscow despt 116 with minute by Drinkall NS 1022/91	8 Dec	Comments on Khrushchev's 'present frame of mind and intentions'; Drinkall thought Khrushchev wanted 'a "face saving" formula about Berlin'.

Quadripartite Rights and Responsibilities, February-December 1960

During the late autumn of 1959 considerable progress was made towards achieving a summit on the lines envisaged by Macmillan. The Prime Minister met with Eisenhower, the French President, General Charles de Gaulle, and the Federal German Chancellor, Konrad Adenauer, in Paris on 19-21 December and, as a result of their deliberations and subsequent exchanges with Moscow, Khrushchev agreed to participate in a four-power summit in Paris opening on 16 May 1960. Preparatory talks amongst the Western leaders were, however, to reveal marked differences over what exactly the summit was meant to achieve. Disarmament, Berlin and other German issues seemed likely to be the main subjects under discussion. But, as Adenauer emphasised in conference with Eisenhower, de Gaulle and Macmillan on 15 May, from Bonn's point of view controlled disarmament was the main question and Western negotiators should not allow Khrushchev to put the German and Berlin problems into the forefront. Despite protests from Eisenhower and Macmillan that it was difficult to see how the Western powers could continue to supply Berlin if the Russians chose to interrupt communications by a 'series of actions falling short of what could be qualified a casus belli', Adenauer maintained that 'the balance of power in Europe and, therefore, in the world was involved in the fate of Berlin' and that Khrushchev would know that a renewal of the Berlin blockade would involve a risk of war. Khrushchev, who had again raised the spectre of the Soviet Union signing a peace treaty with the GDR, was, he contended, 'bluffing' (No. 199).

Adenauer need not have worried. The Paris summit was over almost before it began. On 1 May an American U-2 reconnaissance aircraft had been shot down above Soviet territory, and at a preliminary meeting with the Western leaders on 16 May Khrushchev repeated earlier demands for a halt to such flights, an American apology, and a promise to punish those responsible. Khrushchev refused to accept as adequate a statement by Eisenhower that such flights had been suspended and would not be resumed, and left Paris on the 18th for East Berlin. He nonetheless indicated that he hoped for a further summit meeting in six to eight months' time, though he again threatened to conclude a peace treaty with the GDR. Macmillan was personally doubtful about the prospects for a further summit. Given the way Eisenhower had been treated at Paris, he thought it unlikely that negotiations at that level could recommence even within a year. Rather, he considered it better for the Western powers to concentrate on strengthening their alliance, particularly with a view to agreeing on 'some constructive solution for Berlin which would remove the weapon which [their] exposed position there [gave] to the Russians' (No. 200). In the short term, the British wanted to keep Berlin quiet. They were thus anxious that the West Germans should not, through political actions or legislative measures, afford the Russians an opportunity to challenge the occupation status of the city. The Bonn Government's wish to hold the opening session of the *Bundestag*, the lower house of the Federal German parliament, in Berlin in the autumn of 1960 might, it was feared, provoke such a reaction (Nos. 201-03 & 205). And although Lord Home, who succeeded Selwyn Lloyd as Foreign Secretary in July 1960, appeared not unsympathetic to the eventual transformation of West Berlin into a free city, provided that through the employment of UN troops it 'remained genuinely free', he was reluctant to contemplate any fresh initiative before the US presidential elections in the autumn (No. 204).

The Western allies could not wholly ignore the capacity of the East Germans to make trouble for them. In August new restrictions were imposed on West Berliners and allied military missions in the East had to reckon with a raft of obstructive measures. Nonetheless, Hoyer Millar, who was now PUS, remained of the opinion that the Western powers must be careful to avoid precipitating a crisis or embarking on action from which they might suffer more than the East Germans. In a minute to Home of 1 October, he argued that the West should 'be very hesitant about bringing the German or Berlin issues before the UN or of making speeches or tabling resolutions about them'. This, he added, 'might only "hot things up" unnecessarily, and lead to unfortunate interventions or proposals by the neutrals' (No. 206). It was, however, generally accepted that once a new administration was in place in Washington the Soviet Government would move on the Berlin question, and with this in mind British officials began work on a paper setting out the options for a settlement (Nos. 207-08). The paper, which Sir Evelyn Shuckburgh, Deputy

Under-Secretary of State (DUS) in the Foreign Office, submitted to Hoyer Millar on 16 November, restated the fundamental Western position on Germany in general and Berlin in particular. 'We refuse recognition of the Communist regime in East Germany', it asserted, 'as part of our refusal to accept the final division of Europe by force along the lines of the Iron Curtain, and because we uphold the principles that Germany's future should be determined by free choice of the German people and reunification brought about by means of free elections.' The loss of Berlin would destroy what was left of the West's authority to further these principles. But the paper also pointed out that the *status quo* could not be preserved if the Russians were determined to change it, and that the question was whether a solution could be negotiated which would place the West in a better position than if it stood on its rights and resisted Soviet and East German pressures. The 'least damaging solution', it concluded, would be 'some kind of "free city" with real guarantees and covering if possible the whole of Berlin' (No. 209).

In preparing this paper Shuckburgh was very conscious of the importance of saying nothing which might risk forfeiting Washington's support by urging upon the US 'a "soft" policy over Berlin'. The triumph of the Democratic candidate, Senator John F Kennedy, in the US presidential elections in November, meant that the incoming administration would be strongly committed to impressing on Moscow the strength of the West's commitment to maintaining its stake in Berlin. Moreover, it was unlikely that Adenauer would be in any position to consider any concessions on Berlin or the GDR before the Federal German parliamentary elections in September 1961 (*ibid.*). It was therefore hardly surprising that Sir Harold Caccia, the British Ambassador in Washington, endorsed Shuckburgh's recommendation that HMG's immediate task must be to secure a further postponement of the Soviet threat to sign a separate peace treaty (No. 210). Caccia and other British Heads of Mission also agreed that in negotiations with the Russians HMG should endeavour to prevent Berlin being the only subject under discussion and 'should try to submerge it in other topics' (No. 213). But Sir Pierson Dixon, the newly-appointed British Ambassador in Paris, challenged conventional wisdom when in a letter of 8 December he suggested that the continued division of Germany might provide the best basis for the future stability of Europe (No. 211). Sir Frank Roberts, Britain's Ambassador in Moscow, likewise thought that Western governments had better be clear about what they would concede in any negotiations on Berlin. Khrushchev, he assumed, would reopen the question in the spring of 1961 and, faced by the prospect of his concluding a separate peace treaty with the GDR, the West would choose to negotiate (No. 212).

DOCUMENT SUMMARIES

	DOCUMENT	DATE	MAIN SUBJECT
198	Minute by Sinclair WG 1015/47	**1960** 10 Feb	Examines legal status of Berlin and its relationship with the FRG.
199	Paris tel 170 PREM 11/3005	15 May	Summarises meeting at which Adenauer criticised Soviet proposals on Berlin.
200	Minute: Macmillan to	24 May	Predicts that Khrushchev was

	Home PREM 11/3346		bound to return to the charge over Berlin: HMG's first task must be 'to strengthen the Western alliance as far as possible'.
201	Letter: Marten to Tomkins WG 1015/119	2 July	Discusses French anxieties about FRG encroachment on allied rights, and attaches draft working paper on status of Berlin.
202	Letter: Tomlinson to Marten WG 1015/126	18 July	Comments on No. 201.
203	Minute: Home to Macmillan WG 0122/22	8 Aug	Suggests that a decision not to hold *Bundestag* meeting in Berlin would be regarded as a defeat for the West and a success for Khrushchev's policy of threats.
204	Minute: Home to Macmillan WG 1015/105	8 Aug	Covers memo on the problem of Berlin. Home liked the idea of a free city protected by UN troops, but argues no initiative could be taken before the US election.
205	Bonn tel 211 Saving WG 0122/30	25 Aug	Considers proposed *Bundestag* meeting in Berlin: 'we should try and keep out of this if we can'.
206	Minute: Hoyer Millar to Home WG 1015/171	1 Oct	Argues that Western allies must be prepared to negotiate with Russians on Germany and Berlin, and be careful not to precipitate a crisis.
207	Letter: Thomson to Killick WG 1015/168	6 Oct	Reports that State Dept appreciate case for restraint, but feel counter-measures should be taken to deter Khrushchev over Berlin.
208	Minute: Shuckburgh to Hoyer Millar WG 1015/183	20 Oct	Argues that it was 'very dangerous' to give the impression of wanting a summit.
209	Minute: Shuckburgh to Hoyer Millar WG 1015/193	16 Nov	Submits paper on Berlin: 'How soon the crisis will come and how severe it will be depends on Mr Khrushchev.'
210	Letter: Caccia to Shuckburgh WG 1015/194	6 Dec	Comments on No. 209 in respect of US attitude towards Berlin.
211	Letter: Dixon to Shuckburgh WG 1015/194	8 Dec	Comments on No. 209 and French attitude towards Berlin.

212	Letter: Roberts to Shuckburgh WG 1015/194	14 Dec	Comments on No. 209: pressure from Communist parties made it difficult for Khrushchev to 'leave the Berlin question simmering for very much longer'.
213	Minute by Shuckburgh WG 1015/208	23 Dec	Summarises views expressed on No. 209: 'we must always give the Germans the feeling that reunification is there at the end of the tunnel'.
214	Minute: Home to Shuckburgh WG 1015/208	27 Dec	Speculates on whether Khrushchev might be content with an 'interim solution'.
215	Letter: Dean to Shuckburgh WG 1015/194	28 Dec	Agrees in general with No. 209: UN debate on Berlin would be undesirable.

Security Issues, January-August 1961

Khrushchev left Western diplomats in no doubt over his intentions regarding Berlin. In conversation with the West German Ambassador in Moscow he expressed some optimism regarding future relations with President Kennedy, but he also made plain his determination to settle the Berlin problem in 1961 (No. 216). In these circumstances it was essential that the Western allies settle their as yet unresolved differences over how they should react to unilateral Soviet action. Neither the Americans nor the British believed that the Russians wanted war over Berlin. While, however, the Americans argued that limited military action along the Autobahn could call the Russians' bluff and either restore allied access, or at least bring the Russians to negotiate, the British considered it vital to avoid confronting Khrushchev with a situation in which he was 'faced with the direct choice between climbing down with loss of face or meeting force with force'. If the East Germans imposed unacceptable conditions or obstructed allied land access to Berlin, then the British favoured responding with an airlift—a course which the Americans considered 'unacceptably weak'. As a result of these differences, contingency plans had been prepared, a number of which the British Chiefs of Staff regarded as 'dangerous military nonsense', and no allied commitment had yet been made to any particular plan (No. 218). Allied contingency planning was in the words of Sir Christopher Steel, the British Ambassador in Bonn, 'getting into a complicated and over organised mess' (No. 223).

A visit to Washington in early April left both Macmillan and Home under the clear impression that, while the Americans might be prepared to accept the *de facto* existence of the GDR, they believed that if there were substantial and continuing interference with land communications with Berlin the Western powers should be ready to undertake at once a military operation on a substantial scale. Its object 'would be to stage a real test of will, the assumption being that since the Soviet Union [did] not want war over Berlin, they would see that the situation did not arise' (No. 219). Home, who felt fairly certain that Khrushchev would take an initiative in the autumn, would have preferred Western governments to make the first move by proposing fresh negotiations on Berlin. 'The whole question', he wrote to Macmillan on 27 May, 'really turns on whether the West is prepared to risk nuclear war for the defence of its position in Berlin.' In any event, Home thought that Khrushchev was clearly aware of the difficulties he and the East Germans could make for the West by appearing reasonable and not initially interfering with allied rights of access (No. 224). That appeared to be borne out by the *aide-mémoire* which Khrushchev presented to Kennedy during talks with the US President in Vienna on 3-4 June. The document simply restated the Soviet position on Berlin and the German question, calling for a peace conference and the establishment of West Berlin as a demilitarised free city.[10] But Kennedy was also perturbed by communist infiltration in Laos, and during his subsequent stay in London both he and Macmillan agreed that for the West to offer negotiations before a Laotian settlement had been achieved 'might seem to be a sign of weakness'. The 'simple position' for the West to take would, Macmillan observed, 'be to say that the Russians could do what they liked about a treaty with the D.D.R., but the West stood on their rights and would meet any attack on these will all the force at their command' (No. 225). This, however, left unresolved the questions of how exactly the Western powers should respond to Khrushchev's latest proposals and what counter-measures they might take in the event of interference with their rights of access.

Home still felt that, even if negotiations were for the moment excluded, the West should express a willingness to discuss with the Soviet Government the problems of Germany including Berlin (No. 226). Meanwhile, the Americans appeared to be working towards possible action on two fronts: the introduction of a series of overt military measures designed to demonstrate that the West was making preparations for a major showdown; and the introduction of the whole issue into the UN on the basis of a reference to the International Court of Justice of the legal point as to whether Western rights could be abrogated by unilateral Soviet action (No. 228). Home was dubious about this latter option, though he conceded that it 'would at least have the value of getting the President off the hook'. American plans for a retaliatory land probe, despatching forces along the Autobahn in the event of Soviet or East German action, were, likewise, viewed with some scepticism by the Chiefs of Staff: they supported a probe and, if it failed, a garrison airlift, but they did not believe that 'tripartite land operations on a battalion or higher level would be successful either from the military or political stand points'. It was in the opinion of Harold Watkinson, the Minister of Defence, therefore important that the Western military position should be cleared up and that this should be done on a quadripartite basis. He also wanted an agreed Western plan for Berlin, the maintenance of the *status quo* being a far from satisfactory basis upon which to threaten a major war (Nos. 229-30). But Macmillan was averse to Watkinson's proposal that Britain might take the initiative in calling for a meeting in Paris of the four Chiefs of Staff and General Lauris Norstad, the Supreme Allied Commander in Europe. If the British were thus to take the lead, the Prime Minister feared they might be thought to be dragging their feet if they ventured on the slightest criticism of American strategy and tactics, and that they could provoke a sterling crisis if they decided on any overt measures (No. 231).

Khrushchev's public stance on Berlin seemed in the meantime to grow increasingly intransigent. And on 17 July the three Western powers responded in separate but similar notes to the *aide-mémoire* delivered to Kennedy in Vienna. In its

[10] Cmnd. 1552, pp. 443-47. Cf. *FRUS 1961-1963*, vol. xiv, pp. 87-98.

note the British Government reaffirmed the legal basis of the allied presence in Berlin and warned the Russians of the dangers of attempting unilaterally to terminate Western rights there. The Western allies also expressed a willingness to consider a freely negotiated settlement of the unresolved problems of Germany, but insisted that such a settlement had to be in conformity with the principle of self-determination and in the interests of all concerned.[11] The British were, however, acutely aware of the need for caution in the messages they gave out. As Home observed in a Cabinet memorandum of 26 July, too much talk of military postures was 'likely to frighten people rather than stiffen them', and too much talk about negotiation would embarrass the Americans and risked encouraging charges that the British were '"soft" on Berlin'. He nevertheless argued that Khrushchev might be deterred from taking unilateral action, possibly at the time of the Soviet Communist Party Congress on 17 October, if some prospect of negotiations on terms which he would think satisfactory, were opened up. Indeed, in outlining the options for such a negotiation, Home even admitted that German reunification was not desired, 'at least for the time being', though he cautioned that the West could not abandon the principle of German self-determination (No. 232). Yet it was evident that no substantive negotiations involving concessions to the Soviet Union could be contemplated before the West German elections on 17 September, and, as was pointed out in Cabinet on 28 July, HMG's 'most immediate aim' must be to ensure that nothing was done to precipitate action by Khrushchev before that date (No. 234).

DOCUMENT SUMMARIES

	DOCUMENT	DATE	MAIN SUBJECT
216	Tel 41 to Bonn LY 10310/6	**1961** 6 Jan	Repeats Moscow tel 34, reporting that Khrushchev was insisting on settlement of the Berlin problem in 1961.
217	Minute by Killick WG 1015/193	1 Feb	Circulates amended version of Shuckburgh's paper (No. 209).
218	Minute by Tomkins CG 1016/4	13 Mar	Comments on differences with the US on contingency planning.
219	Tel 2540 to Washington PREM 11/3347	20 Apr	Seeks clarification of US position on Berlin.
220	Bonn tel 429 PREM 11/3347	30 Apr	Reports Khrushchev's expressed determination 'to reach a solution' of Berlin problem in 1961.
221	Minute: Home to Macmillan PREM 11/3347	11 May	Emphasises need for agreement on ideas before NATO discussions on Berlin.
222	Moscow tel 997	25 May	Reports information from US

[11] Cmnd. 1552, pp. 448-50.

	PREM 11/3347		Ambassador on interview with Khrushchev.
223	Letter: Steel to Shuckburgh CG 1016/30	26 May	Discusses contingency planning, which seemed to be 'getting into a complicated and over-organised mess'.
224	Minute: Home to Macmillan PREM 11/3347	27 May	Contends, with reference to No. 222, West must work out a negotiating position before Khrushchev acts over Berlin.
225	Record of conversation: Macmillan/Kennedy PREM 11/3347	5 June	Discussion of Berlin problem: moral position, negotiating tactics and contingency planning.
226	Minute: Home to Macmillan CG 1016/21	9 June	Attaches note on Berlin, discussing problems raised by Khrushchev's *aide-mémoire* to Kennedy.
227	Washington tel 1431 PREM 11/3347	12 June	Reports on French attitude towards the Berlin problem.
228	Washington tel 1499 PREM 11/3347	18 June	Shuckburgh offers impressions of Home's visit to Washington.
229	Extract from record of conversation: Home/Watkinson CG 1016/44	22 June	Discussion of military planning with regard to Berlin.
230	Minute: Watkinson to Macmillan PREM 11/3348	23 June	Registers concern about politico-military situation regarding Berlin.
231	Minute: Macmillan to Bishop PREM 11/3348	24 June	Covers draft minute to Home concerning No. 230: 'If nuclear war takes place over Berlin, we shall all be dead.'
232	Memo by Home CAB 129/106	26 July	Sets out possible approach to Berlin problem and basis for negotiation with the Soviet Union.
233	Memo by Watkinson CAB 129/106	27 July	Examines military aspects of the Berlin problem and implications of the military preparations the Americans expect UK to make.
234	Cabinet Conclusions (extract) CAB 128/35	28 July	Records approval of No. 232: 'Our most important immediate aim should be to ensure that no action was taken by our Allies or ourselves to precipitate action by Mr Khrushchev' before German elections.

235	Minute: Strong to Shuckburgh CG 1016/102	1 Aug	Expresses views on Khrushchev's thinking about Germany.

Freedom of Movement, 1959-1961

Early in August 1961, the flow of refugees into West Berlin from the East reached levels unparalleled since the East German rising of 1953, with 20,000 fleeing to the West in less than a fortnight. Between the establishment of the communist régime in East Germany in September 1949 and 31 May 1961, 2,619,061 people left the GDR. The departure of nearly 450,000 of these followed the issue of Khrushchev's notes in November 1958 and, although the flow of refugees to the West fell to less than 150,000 in 1959, during the next year, in the wake of a drive to complete agricultural collectivisation, the number rose to 200,000, and reached 103,159 during the first half of 1961. As the documents in this group confirm, British representatives in the city understood the anxiety of the East German authorities over the increase in refugee numbers and, more particularly, the number of teachers and doctors leaving for the West (No. 246). However, Bernard Ledwidge, Political Adviser to the British Military Government in Berlin, questioned the political significance of these figures. In a letter of 12 December 1960 he contended that the Russians were presumably aware that the East German economy would not be in danger of collapsing if nothing were done in 1961 or 1962 to stem the flow of refugees. He therefore concluded that while the refugee problem was now serious enough to force the Russians to give greater weight to it in considering their Berlin strategy, it would 'not in the next year or two be a decisive factor making for urgency and the running of increased risks if such action [was] inconsistent with the broader objectives of Soviet foreign policy' (No. 248). Moreover, East German restrictions imposed on freedom of movement in Berlin in September 1960 were, in practice, abandoned when the West Germans and the three Western occupying powers threatened to retaliate by halting interzonal trade (No. 250).

The sharp increase in the flow of refugees through Berlin during July and early August 1961 was, however, of considerable concern to British diplomats. They recognised that its primary cause was probably a fear that the escape route might soon be closed. Migration at the levels reached in July seemed bound to damage the economy of the GDR and its prestige abroad, and there was an 'obvious danger' that East German attempts to stem the tide could 'complicate the Berlin problem still further and possibly even precipitate a crisis' (No. 256). Ledwidge even speculated on the 'remote contingency' of civil disturbances in East Germany similar to those of 1953 (No. 253). But in a telegram of 12 August, a day on which the record daily number of 2,400 crossed from East to West, the BMG reported that it did not consider that the population movement would itself precipitate an acute crisis. 'Rather', the BMG concluded, 'we should say that the state of affairs within East Germany increases for Khrushchev the attractiveness of some agreement with the Western Powers as against a unilaterally imposed "settlement" of the German problem' (No. 257).

DOCUMENT SUMMARIES

DOCUMENT	DATE	MAIN SUBJECT

236	Bonn tel 40 Saving WG 1821/2	**1959** 2 Feb	Reports 1958 figures for Soviet zone refugees: 22% down on 1957.
237	Letter: BMG Berlin to Chancery, Bonn WG 1821/2	27 May	Casts doubt on East German press claims regarding refugee figures.
238	Letter: Stretton to Drinkall with minute by Drinkall WG 10110/2	8 Sept	Reports on traffic and 'technical contacts' between East and West Germany.
239	Bonn tel 7 Saving WG 1821/1	**1960** 12 Jan	Reports Soviet zone refugee figures for 1959 lowest since 1949.
240	Berlin despt 9 to Bonn WG 1821/7	11 Mar	Comments on East-West population movement and resulting problems for GDR.
241	GOC Berlin tel 14 Saving WG 1821/10	20 Apr	Reports unusually large seasonal increase in the flow of refugees.
242	GOC Berlin despt 17 to Bonn WG 1821/17	30 June	Analyses refugee flow during 1960 and reversal of steady decline in East-West movement.
243	Record of meeting: Western Commandants and Brandt WG 1018/32	1 Oct	Discussion of problems arising from Soviet obstructive measures.
244	Bonn tel 247 Saving WG 1821/23	14 Oct	Suggests that travel restrictions may have increased refugee flow.
245	Letter: BMG Berlin to Chancery, Bonn WG 1018/37	7 Nov	Reports pressure on Soviet zone residents working in W Berlin, and increase in number of them reporting as refugees.
246	Letter: Buxton to Ledwidge WG 1015/168	28 Nov	Requests views on US assessment that the refugee flow will force the Russians to take a tough line in Berlin negotiations.
247	Letter: BMG Berlin to Chancery WG 1821/27	29 Nov	Reports 'unmistakable signs of anxiety' in GDR over increased number of doctor and teacher refugees.
248	Letter: Ledwidge to Buxton WG 1821/32	12 Dec	Replies to No. 246: 'very serious' problems for the GDR posed by the refugee flow.
249	Bonn tel 55 Saving CG 1821/2	**1961** 27 Mar	Reports 38% annual increase in East German refugees.
250	Bonn despt 99 CG 1622/3	5 June	Examines GDR restrictions on freedom of movement and impact of Western counter-measures.

251	Bonn tel 101 Saving CG 1821/2	9 June	Reports 12% annual decrease in E German refugees in May.
252	BMG Berlin tel 218 CG 1821/6	13 July	Reports sharp rise in flow of refugees into Berlin, reflecting fears of closure of escape route.
253	Letter: Ledwidge to Duff CG 1018/22	27 July	Comments on possible effects of high refugee flow on GDR and Soviet policy on Berlin.
254	Letter: Marten to Tomkins CG 1018/22	2 Aug	Comments on No. 253.
255	Bonn tel 162 Saving CG 1821/2	5 Aug	Reports 84% annual rise in East German refugees in July.
256	Tel 132 to Berlin CG 1821/18	10 Aug	Asks that FO be kept closely informed on refugee flow and its impact on GDR.
257	BMG Berlin tel 270 CG 1821/8	12 Aug	Replies to No. 256: while refugee flow is unlikely to precipitate acute crisis, it may make agreement with Western powers more attractive to Khrushchev.

The Crisis breaks, August 1961

Early on the morning of 13 August 1961 the GDR Government announced new and much stricter controls on the movement of East Germans, including East Berliners, to West Berlin, and proceeded to erect barricades sealing off the Soviet from the Western sectors of the city (No. 258). In this potentially dangerous international situation the British Government was concerned 'that nothing should be said or done by the West to increase the tension or to stimulate uprising in East Germany' (No. 270). Home was reluctant to engage in any action by the Western powers which might invite counter-measures and allow events to escalate out of control. Even a West German proposal for suspending the issue of Temporary Travel Documents (TTDs) to East German citizens was initially opposed on the grounds that, since the GDR was unlikely to lift its latest restrictions, the suspension would become permanent (No. 269). Indeed, Home was inclined to see in the East German move a possible 'peg on which to hang a proposal for talks' leading, he hoped, to a negotiated arrangement which would guarantee the Western position in Berlin and the freedom and viability of West Berlin itself (Nos. 278 & 281). However, agreement was reached at a meeting in Washington on the evening of 15 August between the British, French and West German Ambassadors there and Foy Kohler, the US Assistant Secretary of State for European Affairs (the Ambassadorial Group), on the text of notes, delivered separately in Moscow on the 17th by the Ambassadors of the three Western occupying powers, to the Soviet Government, protesting at the 'flagrant, and particularly serious, violation of the quadripartite status of Berlin' (Nos. 282-83). Faced by mounting criticism, particularly in Germany, of Western inaction, Home was also ready at Washington's behest to undertake certain military measures, including the reinforcement of the British garrison in Berlin and participation in hastening the build-up of NATO forces (No. 294).

The Americans were disappointed that the reinforcement of British forces in Berlin consisted of no more than the despatch of armoured vehicles to the city. They, like the French, were similarly perturbed over the Foreign Office's desire to link a proposed statement by the three Western Heads of Government, affirming their determination to maintain their rights and fulfil their obligations in Berlin, to messages to the Soviet Government indicating their readiness to explore the 'modalities of negotiations' (Nos. 309-12). But from Moscow, Roberts warned Home against a tripartite declaration which might provoke further action or some violent counter-declaration by Khrushchev. Roberts thought it important to 'guard against the danger that the exercise of reassuring the Berliners and maintaining West German morale might take us so far that it forced a response from Khrushchev which would still further increase tension and involve us all in political and possibly military escalation' (No. 313). With this Home evidently agreed. Certainly, he found unacceptable de Gaulle's opinion that a move towards negotiations would be inconsistent with the tough tone of the draft statement, and, in view of divergent British and French views on this issue, Kennedy decided to abandon the tripartite statement (Nos. 315 & 320). West Berliners had meanwhile to make do with a visit from the US Vice-President, Lyndon Johnson, and the despatch to the city of an American battle group. There was no point, Steel noted in a telegram of 21 August, 'in further bolstering Berlin morale, which [was] far too addicted to a diet of gestures' (Nos. 321 & 323). Nor was Steel ready to take too seriously a Soviet note of 23 August protesting at the connivance of the Western allies with West German '[r]evanchists, extremists, subverters, spies and saboteurs' who had been allowed to use their air corridors to Berlin. He estimated that any physical action in the air corridor would appear to Khrushchev as being 'about the most dangerous he could take', and he dismissed the note as part of the general propaganda build-up, designed 'to create a new factitious grievance with an eye to coming negotiations' (Nos. 325 & 331).

That there would be negotiations Home seems not to have doubted. In a Cabinet memorandum of 1 September he predicted a 'very tough and difficult' negotiation before the end of the year. And to that end he supported Kennedy's efforts to increase American military preparedness and measures to strengthen NATO (No. 332). In fact, however, with the sealing off of East from West Berlin the prospect of negotiations receded. *Bundestag* elections on 17 September diminished Adenauer's authority, forcing him eventually into a coalition with the FDP and delaying the achievement of any common Western negotiating position. Moreover, on 17 October, at the Soviet Communist Party Congress, Khrushchev withdrew his deadline for the signing of a peace treaty,[12] and for the time being there were no more public references by the East German leader, Walter Ulbricht, to the transformation of West Berlin into a neutralised free city. As Steel subsequently noted, the construction of a wall separating East from West 'removed a great deal of Berlin's sting from the Soviet point of view'.[13] Nonetheless, the Berlin wall by no means solved the problems of the GDR, and the divided city remained a potential source of conflict. 'The continuous survival of West Berlin as a thriving outpost of

[12] Cmnd. 6201, *Selected Documents on Germany and the Question of Berlin 1963-1973* (London: HMSO, 1975), pp. 36-37.

[13] *FRG: Annual Review for 1961*, Bonn despatch No. 1 of 2 January 1962, CG 1011/1.

the Western world in the middle of the DDR must', observed Major-General Rohan Delacombe, the General Officer Commanding the British sector, 'be regarded by Herr Ulbricht as an intolerable obstacle to his regime's consolidation and as a permanently unsettling factor. The reflection of the bright lights of West Berlin is still visible even across the Wall, the very existence of which enhances the poignancy and attractiveness of the sight.'[14]

DOCUMENT SUMMARIES

	DOCUMENT	DATE	MAIN SUBJECT
258	BMG Berlin tel 271 CG 10113/11	**1961** 13 Aug	Announces much stricter controls on movement of East Germans, including East Berliners, to West Berlin.
259	BMG Berlin tel 272 CG 10113/12	13 Aug	Reports sharp decrease in refugee flow.
260	BMG Berlin tel 275 CG 10113/12	13 Aug	Informs that Commandants had decided against joint press statement.
261	Washington tel 1914 CG 10113/14	13 Aug	Reports Rusk's press statement on Berlin had been set in 'low key' to avoid inflaming feelings.
262	Washington tel 1915 CG 10113/14	13 Aug	Transmits Rusk's press statement.
263	SACEUR tel SH29658 CG 10113/21	14 Aug	Reports on Soviet and GDR military deployments in Berlin.
264	Record of meeting at *Kommandatura*: Western Commanders/Amrehn/Klein CG 10112/19	14 Aug	Amrehn registers disappointment of Berliners at absence of Western counter-measures.
265	Bonn tel 777 CG 10113/16	14 Aug	Records discussion between von Brentano and Western Ambassadors on developments in Berlin.
266	Moscow tel 1499 CG 10113/19	14 Aug	Reasons that Khrushchev's actions implied that he was 'ready to be pretty ruthless' if there were uprisings in GDR.
267	Paris tel 463 CG 10113/20	14 Aug	Reports de Carbonnel's views on Western protests.

[14] *Review of Developments in East Germany in 1961*, GOC Berlin despatch No. 7 E(S) to Bonn of 8 March 1962, CG 1011/2.

268	Bonn tel 781 CG 10113/18	14 Aug	Argues that West should use new situation as a 'peg for negotiation'.
269	Tel 1555 to Bonn CG 10113/16	14 Aug	Doubts wisdom of imposing ban on TTDs.
270	Tel 5493 to Washington CG 10113/14	14 Aug	Shuckburgh sends guidance for a meeting of the Ambassadorial Group.
271	Washington tel 1923 CG 10113/22	14 Aug	Reports that Kohler had urged the necessity of a written protest to the Soviet Commandant.
272	Bonn tel 785 CG 10113/16	15 Aug	Contends that HMG would be in difficulties if it confined itself to protests.
273	Tel 145 to BMG Berlin CG 10113/16	15 Aug	Agrees that protest to Soviet Commandant should be made that day, subject to amendments.
274	Paris tel 465 CG 10113/22	15 Aug	Reports French reluctance to agree to ban of TTDs.
275	Bonn tel 787 CG 10113/16	15 Aug	Reports that FRG Government is urging calm on West German population and assuring them that necessary counter-measures are being prepared.
276	Bonn tel 788 CG 10113/16	15 Aug	Questions tactics outlined in No. 273.
277	BMG Berlin tel 283 CG 10113/24	15 Aug	Expresses wish to send message to Soviet Commandant requesting immediate re-opening of Brandenburg Gate.
278	Tel 5517 to Washington CG 10113/27	15 Aug	Argues that it would be appropriate to protest in both Berlin and Moscow.
279	BMG Berlin tel 285 CG 10113/22	15 Aug	Suggests refusing TTDs to GDR officials, propagandists, and sport or cultural representatives.
280	Bonn tel 790 CG 10113/24	15 Aug	Questions wisdom of proposal in No. 277.
281	Tel 5518 to Washington CG 10113/52	15 Aug	Maintains objections to banning the issue of TTDs.
282	Washington tel 1936 CG 10113/26	15 Aug	Reports allied agreement on text of protest to Soviet Government.

283	Washington tel 1937 CG 10113/26	15 Aug	Transmits text reported in No. 282.
284	Washington tel 1938 CG 10113/22	15 Aug	Reports Ambassadorial Group discussion: US favoured none of the measures so far suggested and set out alternatives.
285	Bonn tel 791 CG 10113/22	16 Aug	Notes agreement with No. 279.
286	BMG Berlin tel 288 CG 10113/16	16 Aug	Reports poor press reception of delivery of Commandants' letter to Karlshorst.
287	Minute by Ramsbotham CG 1016/77	16 Aug	Sets out agenda for an urgent meeting, called by Watkinson, to consider military build-up in Berlin.
288	Tel 5541 to Washington CG 10113/22	16 Aug	Expresses agreement with a selective ban on issue of TTDs.
289	Minute: Watkinson to Macmillan CG 1016/97	16 Aug	Reports on meeting to discuss military build-up.
290	Tel 155 to BMG Berlin CG 10113/24	16 Aug	Stresses need to insist on point of entry from British to Soviet sector.
291	BMG Berlin tel 291 CG 10113/30	16 Aug	Reports that Berliners had 'been shaken to a greater extent than ever since 1948'.
292	Moscow tel 1514 CG 10113/22	16 Aug	Agrees that USSR is unlikely to be much impressed by 'pin-pricks' like a ban on TTDs.
293	Bonn tel 794 CG 10113/36	16 Aug	Argues objectives should be: (1) to back up W German customs and frontier guards in dealing with any incident; and (2) to exercise a steadying influence by presence of British troops.
294	Tel 5553 to Washington CG 1016/85	16 Aug	Informs of planned military deployments.
295	Bonn tel 796 CG 10113/16	16 Aug	Reports that 'general atmosphere here [FRG] is still very worked up'.
296	Letter: Kennedy to Macmillan CG 10113/43	17 Aug	Urges the issue of a joint declaration.
297	BMG Berlin tel 292 CG 10113/24	17 Aug	Reports on British measures to protect Soviet war memorial.

298	Bonn tel 799 CG 10113/41	17 Aug	Notes Adenauer's efforts to lower the temperature.
299	Bonn tel 801 CG 10113/41	17 Aug	Reports on Adenauer's meeting with Smirnov
300	BMG Berlin tel 297 CG 10113/88	17 Aug	Records meeting with Brandt, who was 'positive and reasonable'.
301	Letter: Shuckburgh to Strong CG 1016/102A	17 Aug	Expresses disagreement with Strong's paper on Khrushchev's diplomacy.
302	Washington tel 1960 CG 10113/40	18 Aug	Reports Kennedy's decision to reinforce US garrison in Berlin and other measures.
303	Moscow tel 1531 CG 10113/52	18 Aug	Reports Soviet note rejecting Western protests.
304	Moscow tel 1532 CG 10113/52	18 Aug	Transmits translation of Soviet note.
305	Minute by Henderson CG 10113/77	18 Aug	Argues that 'there is no reason to suppose that the imposition of the Berlin frontier controls betokens a deliberate acceleration in the Soviet timetable for the solution of the Berlin problem'.
306	Bonn tel 805 CG 10113/48	18 Aug	Reports that Berlin morale is low but life 'looked surprisingly normal'.
307	Paris tel 472 CG 10113/22	18 Aug	States French were in favour of a total ban on TTDs.
308	BMG Berlin tel 300 CG 10113/24	18 Aug	Points out 'we have no right to send patrols into East Berlin'; but aimed to send 2-3 staff cars in each day.
309	Tel 5634 to Washington CG 10113/43	18 Aug	Transmits message from Macmillan to Kennedy suggesting a declaration could be counter-productive.
310	Tel 5635 to Washington CG 10113/43	18 Aug	Informs that Home wanted it to be clear that UK was fulfilling existing obligations to the people of West Berlin, rather than undertaking new ones.
311	Paris tel 477 CG 10113/43	18 Aug	Relays de Gaulle's reply to Kennedy: he agrees to join in a declaration, but urges caution.
312	Washington tel 1976 CG 10113/43	19 Aug	Reports US disappointment that HMG was not prepared to send reinforcements to Berlin beyond

			armoured vehicles.
313	Moscow tel 1534 CG 10113/45	19 Aug	Urges restraint by Western governments to avoid provoking escalated Soviet response.
314	BMG Berlin tel 306 CG 10113/47	19 Aug	Provides translation of Soviet reply to Commandants' letter.
315	BMG Berlin tel 307 CG 10113/47	19 Aug	Comments on No. 314, which 'contains little besides the familiar catalogue of Western misdeeds.
316	Tel 5652 to Washington CG 10113/43	19 Aug	Agrees with de Gaulle that joint declaration is a serious step.
317	Tel 5664 to Washington CG 10113/58	19 Aug	Transmits personal message from Home to Rusk: states that HMG's main concern is to maintain Western access to West Berlin.
318	Tel 5665 to Washington CG 1016/87	19 Aug	Shuckburgh repeats German Ambassador's worries about ostentatious US reinforcement taking place along the Autobahn.
319	BMG Berlin tel 304 CG 10113/46	19 Aug	Reports on the restrictions at East-West Berlin border.
320	Washington tel 1981 CG 10113/43	19 Aug	Reports that Kennedy had dropped the idea of a tripartite statement.
321	UKDEL NATO tel 109 CG 1016/86	19 Aug	Reports that US delegation informed NAC of the sending of Vice-President and General Clay to Berlin, and discussed the passage of the US Battlegroup.
322	BMG Berlin tel 308 CG 10113/39	19 Aug	Argues that there is an adequate British 'presence' on the Autobahn.
323	Bonn tel 818 CG 10113/43	21 Aug	Expresses pleasure that the idea of a declaration has been dropped.
324	BMG Berlin tel 316 CG 10113/74	23 Aug	Reports on new East German restrictions on border crossings.
325	Moscow tel 1551 CG 1381/12	23 Aug	Relays Soviet note complaining of activities carried out in Berlin by FRG.
326	BMG Berlin tel 320 CG 10113/74	23 Aug	Reports that Western Commandants were agreed that there was no question of complying with GDR instructions to remain 100m from sector border.
327	Tel 5809 to Washington	24 Aug	Suggests Soviet note could be an

	CG 1381/52		attempt to shift blame for recent action by GDR on to Western powers and FRG.
328	Washington tel 2043 CG 1381/13	24 Aug	Reports on the drafting of identical notes for delivery by British, French and US Ambassadors in Moscow.
329	Washington tel 2063 CG 1381/13	25 Aug	Informs of agreed text of notes to the Soviet Government.
330	Washington tel 2064 CG 1381/13	25 Aug	Transmits texts covered by No. 329.
331	Bonn tel 846 CG 1381/52	26 Aug	Contends that Soviet note about corridors was part of a 'general propaganda build-up', designed to create new 'factitious grievance' with an eye to coming negotiations.
332	Cabinet memo by Home C(61)132 CAB 129/102	1 Sept	Summarises current situation regarding Berlin: Khrushchev was 'in a thoroughly overweaning and dangerous frame of mind'.

CHAPTER III
Berlin Reunited
1988-1990

The status of Berlin under four-power occupation was always intimately bound up with questions relating to the future of a divided Germany, and these in their turn could not be addressed without reference to the post-war division of Europe. The new mood of East-West détente, which emerged in Europe during the late 1960s, seemed therefore almost inevitably to impact upon the city. The appointment of the former Social Democrat *Regierender Bürgermeister* of West Berlin, Willy Brandt, first as Federal German Foreign Minister in 1966, and then, three years later, as Chancellor, heralded the adoption of a West German *Ostpolitik* designed to break out of the diplomatic stalemate of the preceding decades in order to achieve an understanding with the GDR and treaties with Germany's eastern neighbours. Brandt's diplomacy was not always congenial to the British. By 1970 the prospect of Bonn formally recognising the GDR seemed likely once more to threaten the position of the Western allies in Berlin, particularly as regards East German competence over access matters. Senior officials of the Foreign and Commonwealth Office (FCO), the successor department to the Foreign Office, were surprised by the degree of agreement achieved in inner-German talks. Both Sir Denis Greenhill, the PUS and Sir Thomas Brimelow, the responsible Deputy Under-Secretary (DUS), contended that Brandt's *Ostpolitik* was putting at risk Britain's interests in the German question and also its position in Berlin.[1] Meanwhile, talks between the four occupying powers, which opened at ambassadorial level in March 1970, resulted in the signing on 3 September 1971 of a Final Stage Quadripartite Agreement on Berlin. This came close to meeting the essential requirements of Britain and its Western allies insofar as they secured a Soviet undertaking that civilian traffic between the Western sectors of the city and the FRG would be unimpeded, recognition that non-political ties between the FRG and the Western sectors would be maintained and developed, Soviet acceptance of West Germany's responsibility for the representation of the Western sectors abroad, and a promise of improvements in inner-Berlin communications. In return, the Russians obtained a reduction of the FRG's political presence in Berlin, an appreciable enhancement of the status of the GDR, and tacit acceptance by Western Governments of the permanence of the Berlin wall and the confinement of their interests to their sectors of the city.[2]

The successful conclusion of the Quadripartite Agreement was one of the conditions set by the Western powers for the opening in late 1972 of multilateral preparatory talks for what became the CSCE.[3] The Conference proved a tortuous and protracted negotiation. Its Final Act, which was signed at the thirty-five nation Helsinki summit in August 1975, went some way towards confirming, without legally endorsing, the territorial *status quo* in Europe.[4] 'For Berliners', noted Major-General Scott-Barrett, the British General Officer Commanding in Berlin, 'this all seem[ed]

[1] Series III, Volume I, pp. 242-43.

[2] *Ibid.*, pp. 376-77. Cmnd. 6201, pp. 236-48.

[3] Series III, Volume II, Nos. 1 and 17-38.

[4] The full text of the Final Act of the CSCE is printed in Cmnd. 6932, pp. 225-82.

to confirm the unsavoury truth implied by the Eastern Treaties that the division of Germany [was] here to stay.' But the CSCE also extended the scope of détente well beyond the notion of an easing of East-West tensions and its Final Act offered new opportunities for transcending the ideological divide of which Berlin was so potent a symbol. Its 'Basket III' measures, particularly those relating to human contacts and access to information, provided Western diplomats and the citizens of the communist régimes of the East with a *locus standi* for pressing for practical changes which would eventually yield greater freedom of movement and expression. Quite how this would affect West Berlin in its relations with the GDR remained uncertain. The East German authorities made it clear that they would resist further pressure from the West. If, however, détente and the West's recognition of the GDR rendered Berlin's role 'much more distant and illusory', the CSCE and its follow-up machinery offered encouragement to those seeking to weaken Moscow's grip elsewhere in Eastern Europe.[5] It was developments there and in the Soviet Union itself that in the following decade were to bring Berlin back into the limelight of international diplomacy.

Berlin remained a potential trouble spot. But when new fronts opened in the Cold War, first in southern Africa and then in Afghanistan, and détente slipped out of fashion, it was the birth of popular reformist movements in Eastern Europe, especially Solidarity in Poland, which captured the attention of governments and public opinion in the West. Meanwhile, the deployment of new missile systems, the upgrading of others, and the escalating costs of superpower rivalry weighed heavily on a Soviet command economy which was already struggling to generate sustained growth and which, by the mid-1980s, was failing to take advantage of the latest advances in information technology. Mikhail Gorbachev's appointment as General Secretary of the Soviet Communist Party in March 1985 gave impetus to the introduction of measures for the economic and political liberalisation of the Soviet Union in the shape of *glasnost* (political openness) and *perestroika* (economic restructuring). These complemented changes already taking place in parts of Eastern Europe and British diplomats began to assume a more proactive approach towards the region. In September 1985 Sir Geoffrey Howe, the Secretary of State for Foreign and Commonwealth Affairs in Margaret Thatcher's Conservative Government, set as an aim of British foreign policy the weakening of the Soviet Union's control over its satellites and their 'gradual evolution away from the current Soviet pattern'. This, in practice, meant encouraging political and economic reform in individual countries while holding out the prospect of economic assistance if that were achieved. It also recognised the existence of a 'creative ferment' in Eastern Europe which would ultimately undermine Soviet power there and reopen questions relating to the future of Germany as a whole and Berlin in particular.[6]

[5] Series III, Volume II, Nos. 137 and 140, and pp. 486-92.

[6] Howe defined British objectives in despatch DD 1985/333 to Warsaw of 5 September 1985, signed for him by John Birch, the Head of the Eastern European Department. In this he argued: 'We should encourage creative ferment in Eastern Europe which brings the Soviet Union to raise the level of its tolerance and which underlines the attractions of Western society. This ferment should be constantly but quietly challenging the dominant role of the Communist Party and the authority of the Soviet Union' (EN 021/11).

Berlin – What Next? January-December 1988

On 12 June 1987, during a visit to the Brandenburg Gate to mark the 750th anniversary of the foundation of Berlin, the US President, Ronald Reagan, delivered a speech in which he challenged the Soviet Union to end the division of Europe. 'General Secretary Gorbachev', he appealed, 'if you seek peace, if you seek prosperity for the Soviet Union and Eastern Europe, it you seek liberalization: Come here to this gate! Mr Gorbachev, open this gate! Mr Gorbachev, tear down this wall!' The presidential rhetoric was accompanied by more mundane proposals for Soviet cooperation with the Western allies in improving commercial air services in Berlin, the hosting of more international meetings in the city, and the sponsoring of youth exchanges and cultural and sporting events.[7] These were subsequently formalised and incorporated in an *aide-mémoire* which the Western allies presented to the Russians in the following December.[8] The Soviet reply was tardy and almost wholly negative in tone. Moscow informed the Western allies in September 1988 that matters relating to East Berlin were for the GDR, not the Soviet Union, and that there was no real demand for increased air links with the city. All that the Soviet Government was prepared to offer was consultations on certain questions relating to Berlin.[9] Meanwhile, however, there were increasing signs that the public in the Federal Republic and Berlin expected change. Eberhard Diepgen, West Berlin's *Regierender Bürgermeister*, maintained his own *Einladungspolitik* (invitations policy), seeking through cross-border visits to better relations with the leadership of the GDR—a policy which, as Sir Julian Bullard, the British Ambassador in Bonn, understood, threatened to erode further the Western stance on the status of East Berlin. For his part, Bullard felt that provided the Western allies did not concede the fundamentals of their position, they 'should try to accommodate German aspirations for the Wall to become more "permeable" and for Berlin to play a part in the development of East/West relations' (No. 333).

British policy with regard to Berlin continued to be based upon constants that had obtained since 1945: the defence of allied rights and responsibilities in the face of Soviet intransigence and opportunism, combined with the maintenance of a pragmatic quadripartite working relationship. There were still inter-allied tensions, particularly in 1988 over proposed changes to air schedules, but the British kept their nerve by arguing for stability and outfacing the Americans, who had been resorting to 'bullying tactics' (Nos. 336 & 339). Nevertheless, at a time when relations between the superpowers were in flux and when pressures for economic, political and social reform were mounting in Eastern Europe, the British adopted a distinctly cautious attitude towards the prospect of anything more than modest change in Berlin. In a valedictory letter of 20 December Major-General Patrick Brooking, the retiring British Commandant in Berlin, observed that, even if the wall were to become more permeable and central European conventional force reductions put in hand, West Berlin was the 'last place where a military presence ... should be altered or dismantled in a hurry'. He added that it could be argued 'that with so much at stake and with so much uncertainty so close at hand

[7] *Public Papers of the Presidents of the United States: Ronald Reagan, 1987* (United States Government Printing Office: Washington, 1989), vol. i, pp. 634-38.

[8] UKDEL NATO telegram No. 399 of 11 December 1987; undated draft *aide-mémoire* for delivery by the three allies to Soviet Union [preferably] by Chiefs of Mission in Moscow to Foreign Ministry (WRL 021/1). The *aide-mémoire* was delivered on 29 December 1987.

[9] Soviet *aide-mémoire* of 15 September 1988, delivered to the British Embassy, Moscow (WRL 020/3).

geographically, there should be no change to our present posture for some time to come, except perhaps for a light touch or two on the tiller' (No. 341).

DOCUMENT SUMMARIES

	DOCUMENT	DATE	MAIN SUBJECT
333	Letter: Bullard to Dain WRL 014/3	**1988** 22 Jan	Re-examines rationale for British policies and actions in Berlin.
334	Letter: Glover to Flower WRL 014/3	9 Feb	Records discussions with CDU leadership on Berlin issues.
335	Teleletter: Smith to Flower WRL 021/3	9 May	Reports first call by Mallaby on Soviet Ambassador in East Berlin: no indication of positive response to Western intiative.
336	Letter: Parker to Powell WRL 184/3	16 June	Reports UK/US differences over Berlin air services.
337	Bonn tel 937 WRL 020/3	21 Sept	Reports inter-allied discussion of negative Soviet response to Western initiative.
338	Minute by British Embassy, Bonn WRL 012/3	8 Nov	Stresses importance of using correct terminology when referring to Berlin.
339	Bonn tel 1135, with minute by Parker WRL 184/3	9 Nov	Notes success over US in negotiating new agreement on Berlin winter air schedules.
340	Letter: Charlton to Wordsworth WRL 020/1	9 Dec	Reports discussion in Brussels at ministerial and Berlin experts' meetings on GDR and inner-German relations.
341	Letter: Brooking to Mallaby WRL 400/1	20 Dec	Offers personal view of developments in Berlin during preceding three years.

The Berlin Wall, January-September 1989

The concluding sessions of the Vienna CSCE follow-up meeting in January 1989 provided Western statesmen with a fitting occasion on which once more to appeal for an end to the Cold War division of Europe and the removal of the Berlin wall. Howe, and his American and West German counterparts, George Shultz and Hans-Dietrich Genscher, all took up the issue.[10] It was equally predictable that Oskar Fischer, the East German Foreign Minister, should have denounced these calls and that on 19 January Erich Honecker, the Chairman of the GDR's Council of State, should have claimed that the wall would remain for fifty to one hundred years, 'as long as the conditions which made it necessary continued to exist' (No. 342). Some

[10] Cm. 649, *Concluding Document of the Meeting at Vienna from 4 November 1986 to 19 January 1989 to follow up the Conference on Security and Co-operation in Europe* (London: HMSO, 1989), p. 63. US Department of State, *Bulletin* (March, 1989), pp. 50-52.

British officials doubted the wisdom of pressing the GDR to dismantle the wall: its removal would destabilise East Germany and would therefore be resisted by Honecker, and this might impede further progress in the development of relations with the FRG and jeopardise Gorbachev's reform programme in the Soviet Union. It was also difficult to see how West Berlin would cope with a mass exodus of refugees (Nos. 343-45, 347, & 350).

Nevertheless, despite some high-profile incidents, including the shooting dead in February of a young East German caught attempting to scale the wall, the principles and practices of GDR border control became increasingly restrained and cautious as the year progressed (Nos. 346 & 348-49). And the more Honecker proclaimed the wall's permanence, the more fragile it appeared. In January twenty would-be emigrants entered the FRG's mission in East Berlin vowing to remain there until arrangements were made for their transit to the West. Their pleas were rejected, but the GDR authorities indicated that their exit applications would be quickly processed, and during the next six months more than 46,000 East Germans were permitted to leave. When, however, in early August a hundred more hopeful emigrants encamped in the West German mission, they were only offered the prospect of immunity from prosecution, and Bonn was forced to suspend public access to its mission (No. 354). Meanwhile, other East Germans began to depart for the West via Hungary and its border with Austria. But for their part, British diplomats remained far from optimistic about the prospects for radical change. 'Gorbachev's "Common European Home" concept', noted Alan Charlton, Deputy Political Adviser in the BMG Berlin, 'does not so far include any plans for modernisation of the Berlin room ... but at present and, one suspects, for the foreseeable future, the Russians appear to regard their interests as best served by keeping their relations with the GDR on an even keel as possible' (No. 356).

DOCUMENT SUMMARIES

	DOCUMENT	DATE	MAIN SUBJECT
342	East Berlin tel 9 WRL 441/2	**1989** 20 Jan	Reports GDR reactions to British and FRG comments in Vienna on the need to remove the wall.
343	Teleletter: Broomfield to Ratford WRL 040/6	25 Jan	Recommends combining pressure on GDR for improvements in human contacts with occasional public reminders that wall must go.
344	Teleletter: Burton to Ratford WRL 040/6	27 Jan	Endorses view expressed in No. 343.
345	Minute: Lance to Rodemark WRL 040/6	6 Feb	Notes public reaction in GDR to Western rhetoric on the Berlin wall.
346	Minute: Lance to Wordsworth WRL 040/4	8 Feb	Comments on inconsistencies in GDR border guards' application of 'order to shoot' policy.
347	Teleletter: Flower to	9 Feb	Comments on Nos. 343 & 344

	Wordsworth WRL 040/6		and FRG views on removal of the wall.
348	Submission: Dain to Ratford, with minute by Gozney WRL 040/2	27 Feb	Recommends EC *démarche* to GDR on shooting incidents at the Berlin wall.
349	Tel 175 to Bonn WRL 040/2	1 Mar	Instructs Ambassador to seek coordinated response by Bonn Group to Berlin wall escape incidents.
350	Letter: Wordsworth to Dain WRL 040/6	2 Mar	Submits paper on implications of dismantling of Berlin wall.
351	Teleletter: Burton to Ratford ESA 021/413	24 May	Argues for caution in involving CSCE in protests about incidents at Berlin wall.
352	Teleletter: Sands to Wordsworth WRL 040/4	15 June	Reports Honecker's interview with US journalists including reference to more restrictive use of *Schiessbefehl*.
353	Letter: Munro to Wordsworth WRL 020/4	23 June	Argues that Honecker's language reveals insecurity about SED's ability to preserve present GDR.
354	Teleletter: Tucker to Wordsworth WRL 020/7	16 Aug	Reports Soviet comment on 28th anniversary of erection of Berlin Wall: tone reflected concern over German immigration to FRG.
355	Minute: Bishop to Wordsworth ESC 020/36	20 Sept	Analyses recent Soviet comment on the Berlin wall: hints of disapproval of GDR stance.
356	Letter: Charlton to Wordsworth ESC 020/36	27 Sept	Comments on No. 355: suspected that Russians had no intention of rocking the boat with GDR over Berlin.

Scene Setting, January-September 1989

British policy with regard to Berlin could not be divorced from wider issues of East-West relations. By 1989 the city's future and that of Eastern Europe seemed to depend ultimately upon the success of Gorbachev's efforts to reform the Soviet system. Certainly, Thatcher was in no mood to allow Berlin to complicate relations with the Soviet Union. When in conversation with her on 12 January Diepgen argued that some way had to be found to bring the special nature of Berlin more directly to Gorbachev's attention, the Prime Minister retorted that the Soviet leader was 'inevitably very much preoccupied with internal problems ... and with reaching a new relationship with the United States', and would prefer 'to keep [the Berlin] front stable'. It was, she added, too early to make a judgement on whether Gorbachev's reforms would succeed or whether the Soviet Union might slip back into Stalinism: 'We should be patient and work for steady if unspectacular improvement in relations, recognising that Mr. Gorbachev has got as much on his plate as he could cope with'. (No. 357) However, Gorbachev's success in nurturing the perception in Western Europe, and particularly amongst West Germans, that the Cold War was over, had implications for the allies in West Berlin. As Michael Burton, the Minister and Deputy Commandant, BMG Berlin, pointed out in a letter to Sir Christopher Mallaby, the British Ambassador in Bonn, the difficulty for the allies was that of persuading Berliners at a popular level that as the threat of an East-West military confrontation receded the allies still had a useful role to play (No. 360). Moreover, elections in Berlin, which resulted in the formation in March of a Red/Green (SDP/Alternative Liste (AL)) administration, threatened further to complicate matters. Although Walter Momper, Diepgen's successor as *Regierender Bürgermeister*, eventually emerged as 'a reassuring figure for the Allies', there was some initial concern amongst Western diplomats in Bonn lest his wish to develop closer cooperation with the GDR risk undermining their position on the status of Berlin (Nos. 358, 363, 365, 370-71 & 374). And, as Mallaby reminded his colleagues, the Bonn Government was 'at best a weak ally in this area; ... [attaching] greater importance to the development of inner-German relations than to the purity of Berlin's status' (No. 377).

George Bush's new administration in Washington was meanwhile eager to press ahead with an allied diplomatic initiative on Berlin aimed at achieving a package of improvements, including freer access to West Berlin's Tegel airport. This necessitated consultations between all four occupying powers as well as discussions between the two German states. But, while the three Western allies had no wish to engage in any talks involving the reconsideration of the 1971 Quadripartite Agreement, the Russians made clear their reluctance to override the objections of the GDR to four-power talks outside its aegis (Nos. 367-69 & 376). Discussions regarding the initiative and possible measures aimed at modernising the role of the Western allies in Berlin appeared, however, to be rendered increasingly irrelevant when set alongside the mounting problems posed by the arrival in West Berlin and the FRG of ever growing numbers of asylum-seekers and 'resettlers' from the East. Discontent with political and economic conditions in the GDR had led to a growing influx of people to West Germany via third countries, which became particularly marked in August, initially from Hungary and then from Czechoslovakia. Hungary's much-publicised decision to tear down its section of the Iron Curtain opened up a tempting escape route for East Germans hoping to find a better life in the West. As thousands of GDR citizens sought asylum in West German embassies in Prague, Budapest and Warsaw, the SED found itself facing a major economic and political crisis. The refugee issue reopened the debate on the question of German unification (Nos. 361, 366, 382 & 385), and by the end of September the Soviet Government seemed ready to contemplate taking forward the Western initiative on Berlin (No. 386).

DOCUMENT SUMMARIES

	DOCUMENT	DATE	MAIN SUBJECT
357	Letter: Powell to Gozney ESC 020/36	**1989** 12 Jan	Reports Thatcher/Diepgen meeting: Thatcher recommended patience in dealing with Gorbachev.
358	Minute: Wright to Hurd	24 Jan	Records visits to East and West

	WRL 020/4		Berlin and contrast between the two.
359	Minute: Wordsworth to Dain WRL 030/1	30 Jan	Notes 'shock result' in Berlin elections and possibility of SPD/AL alliance.
360	Letter: Burton to Mallaby WRL 020/7	3 Mar	Discusses possibility of allied invitation to Gorbachev to visit West Berlin.
361	Letter: Arkwright to Abbott-Watt WRL 243/1	7 Mar	Reports annual doubling of number of resettlers and asylum seekers in West Berlin.
362	Letter: Broomfield to Burton WRL 020/7	9 Mar	Comments on No. 360: GDR reaction to such a visit would almost certainly be 'strongly negative'.
363	Letter: Corbett to Boyd-Carpenter WRL 021/2	15 Mar	Considers affect of SPD/AL coalition on relations between allies and West Berlin government.
364	Letter: Braithwaite to Mallaby WRL 020/7	10 Apr	Comments on Nos. 360 & 362: Gorbachev unlikely to accept if invited to West Berlin.
365	Letter: Mallaby to Ratford WRL 021/2	21 Apr	Reports on discussions regarding future relations with SPD/AL coalition.
366	Letter: Arkwright to Abbott-Watt WRL 243/1	9 May	Reports significant monthly increase in asylum seekers and resettlers from the East.
367	Submission: Synnott to Fretwell & PS WRL 020/4	24 May	Reviews issues to be raised at forthcoming Berlin ministerial meeting.
368	Tel 785 to Moscow WRL 021/5	8 June	Reports on agreement reached between Britain, France, US and West Germans on further approach to the Russians.
369	Tel 786 to Moscow WRL 021/5	8 June	Text of agreed speaking note on Berlin initiative referred to in No. 368.
370	Submission: Synnott to Ratford WRL 020/3	16 June	Expresses dissatisfaction with press statement to be issued after Momper/Honecker meeting on 19 June, which was erosive of Berlin's status.
371	Minute: Gozney to Synnott WRL 020/3	19 June	Refers to position outlined in No. 370, which Howe found 'increasingly ridiculous'.
372	Moscow tel 1153 WRL 021/5	27 June	Reports Soviet reaction to Western allies' *démarche* on Berlin.

373	Teleletter: Flower to Wordsworth WRL 021/5	28 June	Reports Bonn Group discussion and prospect of an approach to the Russians in Berlin.
374	Letter: Burton to Mallaby WRL 011/1	30 June	Reviews first hundred days of 'Red/Green Senat' in Berlin.
375	Letter: Synnott to Burton WRL 370/3	14 July	Invites thoughts on possible 'modernisation' of British approach to Berlin.
376	BMG Berlin tel 126 to Bonn WRL 021/5	27 July	Reports Soviet Embassy's response to Western allies' *démarche* on Berlin.
377	Letter: Mallaby to Burton WRL 011/1	27 July	Replies to No. 374: Bonn 'at best a weak ally' on the status of Berlin.
378	Letter: Burton to Synnott WRL 370/3	3 Aug	Replies to No. 375: allies faced problem of 'image rather than substance' in Berlin.
379	Letter: Charlton to Dinwiddy WRL 370/3	8 Aug	Sends list of suggestions for 'modernisation' of allied role in Berlin.
380	Draft teleletter: Synnott to Dinwiddy and Lamont WRL 021/5	5 Sept	Suggests making progress on Berlin initiative talks through inclusion of FRG and GDR.
381	Minute by Glover WRL 021/5	8 Sept	Argues that proposal in No. 380 is imaginative, but impossible; 'We do not talk to the GDR and the Soviets would not want to talk to the FRG'.
382	East Berlin tel 260 RS 243/2	12 Sept	Reports extensive critical coverage in GDR media of exodus of refugees from Hungary to FRG.
383	Minute: Cooper to Synnott RS 243/2	13 Sept	Suggests message from Hurd to Genscher offering help with managing influx of refugees to FRG.
384	Minute: Synnott to Cooper RS 243/2	14 Sept	Objects to idea of 'open-ended' offer of help to Genscher.
385	Letter: Lamont to Dinwiddy WRL 021/2	22 Sept	Recommends that British assist Berlin authorities in dealing with influx of resettlers.
386	BMG Berlin tel 63 ESC 020/36	30 Sept	Reports Soviet agreement in principle to preparatory talks on Berlin initiative.

Breaching the Wall, October 1989-January 1990

During early October 1989 protestors demanding reform engaged in major demonstrations in East Berlin and other cities of the GDR on a scale not seen since 1953. On the 18th, faced by mounting public unrest and street demonstrations, Honecker stepped down and was succeeded by Egon Krenz (Nos. 387-89). Nine days later Momper told the Berlin House of Representatives (*Abgeordnetenhaus*) that developments in central Europe required Berlin to think and plan as if the wall no longer existed (No. 390). Momper's public stance, particularly with regard to handling the increased flow of refugees, did not, however, always endear him or his colleagues in the *Senat*, Berlin's executive council, to allied representatives who were worried by their touching on fundamental questions of status (No. 398). As Burton observed, 'the unpredictability of the future course of events, and the serious practical consequences for West Berlin [made] it difficult for politicians to come forward with ringing phrases' (No. 397). Meanwhile, Krenz promised a 'turning point' in the affairs of the GDR, and embarked on a programme of limited economic and political reform. But he lacked credibility as a reformer, being too closely associated with the Honecker régime. The whole of East German society seemed in ferment, and the week beginning Monday 6 November 1989 saw 750,000 protesters on the streets again, demonstrating in six main cities.

Momper described events in the GDR as a 'revolution from below' and 'one of the most significant and moving days in German post-war history' (No. 397). The next day, Tuesday, 7 November, the East German Government resigned. On Wednesday the Politburo followed suit, and then on Thursday the SED Central Committee took the decision which effectively signalled the end of the Cold War in Europe: the opening up of the Berlin wall and free travel to the West. Nigel Broomfield, the British Ambassador in East Berlin, reported back to the FCO on the morning of the 10th that he had witnessed 'an historic night' and 'extraordinary scenes of emotions'. He described how 'huge crowds gathered on the eastern side of all crossing points late in the night. The GDR border guards were forced to give way and thousands drove, walked and ran over the border, some still in their night clothes, hardly believing their eyes ... The underlying unity of the city reasserted itself' (No. 401). A decisive change had taken place in the political life of the GDR. 'Unless', Broomfield noted in a telegram of 13 November, 'a cataclysm occurs in the Soviet Union and sets back with it reforms in Poland and Hungary I can not see how a rapid process of growing together of the two German states can be avoided' (No. 408). Officials in Whitehall were more cautious. An FCO guidance telegram of 14 November counselled British missions against being 'drawn into discussion of the German problem'. The first priority, it argued, was for 'people in the GDR to be able to decide their own future in freedom'. The West German authorities had been careful to play down the question of unification, and the FCO concluded that 'speculation about it at this early stage is unlikely to be helpful' (No. 411).

On 16 November Douglas Hurd, the Secretary of State for Foreign and Commonwealth Affairs, visited the wall, where he shook hands with a GDR border guard. Asked whether there would now be a change in the role of the Western allies in Germany and Berlin, Hurd said that the lesson to be drawn was that we should not change without good reason policies which had been successful. But he added a rider: 'We would, however, continue to adapt ourselves in the light of changing circumstances' (No. 414). Circumstances were indeed changing fast. As Broomfield commented on agreements reached between East and West Germany on freedom of travel, the area within which the GDR authorities could dictate the pace and direction of events was 'being constantly eroded under pressure from the East German population and the economic weight of the Federal Republic' (No. 417). The ceremonial opening of the Brandenburg Gate on 22 December in the presence of Helmut Kohl, the Federal German Chancellor, and Hans Modrow, the new Chairman of the GDR's Council of Ministers, would have been almost unthinkable just six months earlier (Nos. 419-20). Colin Munro, the Counsellor in the British Embassy in East Berlin, recalled the oft-repeated words of the West German President, Richard von Weizsäcker, 'the German question remains open so long as the Brandenburg Gate remains closed'. Passage through the Gate was confined to openings in the wall on either side of it and there was still a vast semi-circle of concrete looking westward from the Gate itself, but, Munro noted, 'the gate had been half-opened and the ingredients of a possible answer to the German Question [were] coming into view' (No. 421).

DOCUMENT SUMMARIES

	DOCUMENT	DATE	MAIN SUBJECT
387	East Berlin tel 299 WRE 014/2	**1989** 9 Oct	Reports second night of major anti-government demonstrations in East Berlin and Dresden.
388	East Berlin tel 305 WRE 014/2	11 Oct	Advises of slight decrease in tension, and persistent hard line in Berlin.
389	East Berlin tel 318 WRE 014/2	18 Oct	Reports replacement of Honecker by Krenz.
390	BMG Berlin tel 174 to Bonn WRL 243/1	27 Oct	Informs of Momper's statement that developments in central Europe meant that Berlin must 'think and plan as if the wall no longer existed'.
391	East Berlin tel 54 to JIC WRE 014/2	30 Oct	Reviews week's developments in GDR.
392	BMG Berlin tel 176 to Bonn WRL 021/2	1 Nov	Reports that *Senat* expects huge influx from East Berlin when GDR travel restrictions are eased.
393	East Berlin tel 43 to BMG Berlin WRE 014/2	1 Nov	Reports on anticipated Alexanderplatz demonstration.
394	Tel 75 to BMG Berlin WRL 021/2	2 Nov	Instructs Burton to impress on Momper 'strong desire' for 'prompt and close consulation'.
395	BMG Berlin tel 181 to Bonn WRL 020/3	3 Nov	Notes that Momper estimates that at least 100,000 people would cross into West Berlin during first weekend after travel restrictions were eased.
396	East Berlin tel 356 WRE 014/2	5 Nov	Reports that 'the will of the people [as expressed at the

			Alexanderplatz rally] was for a democratic transformation of the GDR.'
397	BMG Berlin tel 184 to Bonn WRE 014/2C	6 Nov	Assesses concern of West Berlin authorities about 'practical consequences of current developmnents'.
398	Minutes: Cooper/Gozney RS 243/2	7/8 Nov	Recommend offering assistance to Genscher. This Hurd agrees.
399	BMG Berlin tel 186 to Bonn WRL 020/3	8 Nov	Reports on press speculation about how long Krenz could last.
400	BMG Berlin tel 187 to Bonn WRL 020/8	8 Nov	Reports West Berlin *Senat*'s angry reaction to Bonn's refusal to provide extra financial help.
401	East Berlin tel 371 WRE 014/2	10 Nov [wrongly dated 8 Nov]	Describes an 'historic night' of free travel between East and West.
402	BMG Berlin tel 77 WRE 014/2	10 Nov	Reports that next four days 'could be testing'.
403	BMG Berlin tel 79 WRL 243/1	10 Nov	Assesses situation in Berlin with regard to refugees and their future.
404	UKDEL NATO tel 332 WRE 014/2	10 Nov	Reports Political Committee's discussion of Berlin: 'recent developments were a vindication of the values for which the Alliance stood'.
405	BMG Berlin tel 188 to Bonn WRE 014/2	10 Nov	Records Soviet welcome of allied *Kommandatura*'s decision to authorise West Berlin police to maintain order near Brandenburg Gate.
406	BMG Berlin tel 189 to Bonn WRE 014/2	10 Nov	Reports celebrations and speeches from Berlin politicians: new crossing points announced to 'loud and sustained applause'.
407	BMG Berlin tel 192 to Bonn WRE 014/2	11 Nov	Comments on volatile situation in Brandenburg Gate area: and Soviet gratitude for calm allied handling.
408	East Berlin tel 381 WRE 014/2	13 Nov	Notes that the 'last four days mark[ed] a decisive change in the political life of the GDR'.
409	BMG Berlin tel 195 to Bonn WRE 014/2	13 Nov	Reports events and atmosphere in Berlin over 'historic weekend'.
410	BMG Berlin tel 197 to Bonn WRE 014/2	14 Nov	Offers a Soviet view of events in Berlin following lunch with Maximychev, who agreed

			'emphatically' that reunification was not on the agenda.
411	Guidance tel 67 WRE 014/2	14 Nov	Sets out lines to take on recent events: UK welcomed opening of wall and stood by commitments to Germany; reform of GDR the 'first priority'.
412	BMG Berlin tel 198 to Bonn WRL 021/2	15 Nov	Examines implications for West Berlin of removal of GDR travel restrictions.
413	BMG Berlin tel 199 to Bonn WRL 021/2	15 Nov	Reports that Momper felt Berlin was being 'left in the lurch'; and criticised FRG's handling of situation.
414	BMG Berlin tel 203 to Bonn WRL 026/2	16 Nov	Assesses impact of Hurd's visit to Berlin.
415	Teleletter: Charlton to Dinwiddy WRL 020/3	5 Dec	Gives facts and figures on resettlers arriving in West Berlin: notes low morale of East German military.
416	Letter: Charlton to Dinwiddy WRL 027/3	5 Dec	Retells anecdotes relating to the new situation in Berlin.
417	East Berlin tel 441 WRL 020/4	6 Dec	Notes free movement throughout Germany to begin on 1 Jan 1990, when Berlin would, in effect, become a single city again.
418	Teleletter: Charlton to Dinwiddy WRL 012/1	21 Dec	Reports proposals for expanding Western allied access within Berlin.
419	BMG Berlin tel 232 to Bonn WRL 040/2	22 Dec	Reports GDR's cancellation of ceremonial opening of Brandenburg Gate.
420	BMG Berlin tel 235 to Bonn WRL 040/2	22 Dec	Records opening of Brandenburg Gate by Kohl and Modrow as planned.
421	Munro to Wordsworth (WED) WRL 040/2	29 Dec	Describes opening of Brandenburg Gate from an Eastern perspective.
422	East Berlin tel 1 WRE 014/1	**1990** 2 Jan	Reports New Year messages from East German leaders and massive celebration at Brandenburg Gate.
423	BMG Berlin tel 2 to Bonn WRL 040/1	2 Jan	Describes New Year celebrations at Brandenburg Gate.

Four-Power Case Study: Berlin Aviation, January 1989-May 1990

Relations amongst the three Western occupying powers in Berlin did not always run smoothly. During 1988-89, for instance, the British found themselves at odds with both the Americans and the French in their efforts to achieve a radical overhaul of the allied management of Berlin air services. Put simply, the British sought through negotiation to liberalise current controls and secure greater capacity for UK carriers. But France and, in practice if not in theory, the United States, adopted essentially protectionist stances. They were firm and united in their opposition either to the dismantling of the existing regulatory system, or to the modification of the inter-allied agreement concluded in the summer of 1988 which provided their carriers with substantially more extra capacity than British airlines (No. 424). The British, for their part, were, Mallaby assumed, 'suspected of hatching predatory schemes based on the acknowledged competitive strength of British carriers', and of holding over their allies' heads the threat of breaking ranks if they did not get what they wanted (No. 425). Even, however, if the allies were unable to achieve an understanding on a new long-term framework for air services, they were, by the beginning of March 1989, agreed in principle on the maintenance of air schedules (Nos. 428-33). What they had not reckoned with was the challenge soon to be mounted by East and West Germany to the allied monopoly of air services to Berlin.

On 25 April 1989 at a meeting of the Bonn Group, which brought together representatives of the three Western occupying powers and the FRG, the West Germans revealed that the East Germans had indicated a readiness to allow non-corridor air access to Tegel in return for access to West German airports for the GDR airline, *Interflug*. As Mallaby pointed out in a telegram of 26 April, *Lufthansa* 'would get commercial gains out of such a deal but the driving force in the FRG position [was] likely to be political: a big boost for inner German relations' (Nos. 434-35). The West German authorities, excited at the prospect, wanted to respond with an offer of FRG/GDR air links between Frankfurt-am-Main and Leipzig, and Leipzig and Düsseldorf, for the period 1 July to 31 October 1989, as a test of the other side's intentions (No. 437). The proposal went against the position agreed by the Western allies and the FRG prior to the 1987 Berlin initiative, which was to obtain improvements in air access to the city before conceding direct East-West services. Moreover, the allies had no clear indication of Soviet thinking about the use of Tegel and whether Moscow endorsed the GDR's hints of flexibility. And while the British wanted to avoid a showdown with the FRG, especially as their legal position and allied solidarity were not strong on this point, they thought it 'preferable to smoke out the Russians first' (No. 438). Faced, however, with West German determination to proceed with the proposed services and American opposition to them, Mallaby recommended that HMG 'should leave the Americans to make the running' (No. 441).

Pressure for changes to the air régime intensified following the opening of the Brandenburg Gate and the collapse of other barriers to inter-German travel. In late November Mallaby defined allied interests as: (*a*) to maintain the viability of the air corridors as the ultimate lifeline of Berlin; (*b*) to seek improvements for Berliners by expanded air links; and (*c*) to enhance or protect as far as possible the allies' own commercial interests. These, he argued, were interdependent, since if an allied carrier should withdraw its services because of competition from new inner-German routes, that could 'undermine the political case for insisting on maintaining the corridor regime'; and the potential instability of the GDR and in the area around Berlin was such that air access through the corridors had to be maintained. However, he was not blind to the fact that new arrangements were necessary and that there was a need to consider allowing non-corridor civil flights across the inner-German border. There was also likely to be pressure for even more radical changes as the talks (and political situation) developed. It would, after all, be difficult to resist *Lufthansa* flying to Berlin if the Russians made it clear that they had no objections (No. 445). Discussions on the way forward dragged on for several months until the allies drew up their own proposals on aviation and put them to the West Germans on 8 February 1990. These aimed at opening up the Berlin air régime to others, and made clear that the allies were prepared to allow German carriers into Berlin. But this had also to be negotiated with the Russians (Nos. 455-57). The latter were evidently keen to deflect Berlin aviation talks into the two plus four (FRG/GDR, France, UK, US and USSR) framework established for negotiations on German unification. As Burton wrote from Berlin '[Russian] security interests would be directly involved in any changes made in the air corridor regime ... They must, therefore, have concluded that the question should be considered as part of the wider security picture' (No. 460).

DOCUMENT SUMMARIES

	DOCUMENT	DATE	MAIN SUBJECT
424	Submission: Dain to Ratford WRL 184/1	**1989** 10 Jan	Outlines negotiating tactics for forthcoming allied talks on Berlin air services.
425	Bonn tel 55 WRL 184/1	17 Jan	Seeks instructions on key points for final round of Berlin air services talks.
426	BMG Berlin tel 8 WRL 184/1	20 Jan	Stresses that if talks break down, this must not become public just before Berlin elections.
427	Bonn tel 73 WRL 184/1	20 Jan	Insists that British negotiators 'keep on talking past election day'.
428	Bonn tel 123 WRL 184/1	31 Jan	Reports deadlock in negotiations and recommends setting date for resuming discussion of long-term framework.
429	Minute: Dain to Gozney WRL 184/1	1 Feb	Summarises current position on negotiations, which would resume on 1 March.
430	Letter: Siddle to Moss WRL 184/1	1 Feb	Sets out legal position on Berlin air services in the light of failure of negotiations with Americans and French.
431	Tel 109 to Bonn WRL 184/1	3 Feb	Urges that Germans should not get impression UK was to blame for failure to agree in aviation negotiations.
432	Letter: Neville-Jones to Ratford WRL 184/1	7 Feb	*Post-mortem* on Berlin air negotiations.
433	Bonn tel 275	3 Mar	Reports further round of Berlin

	WRL 184/1		air services talks on 1-2 March: French and Americans accepted reluctantly that short- or medium- term agreement was impossible.
434	Bonn tel 453 MRA 184/623/1	26 Apr	Reports FRG presentation of GDR air service proposals to Bonn Group.
435	Bonn tel 454 MRA 184/623/1	26 Apr	Transmits text of FRG report referred to in No. 434.
436	Tel 307 to Bonn MRA 184/623/1	2 May	Informs that proposals in Nos. 434-35 required more thought and must be part of wider package.
437	Bonn tel 473 WRL 184/1	3 May	Reports that FRG wanted to approve *Lufthansa* and *Interflug* flights on a trial basis.
438	Submission: Synnott to Ratford WRL 184/ 1	15 May	Recommends that UK be prepared to accede to FRG's request '*if* they persist'.
439	Bonn tel 565 MRA 184/623/1	26 May	Reports Bonn Group's discussion of proposal for inner-German air services, and US oppostion to separating from Berlin initiative.
440	Bonn tel 709 WRL 021/5	6 July	Recommends reluctant UK agreement to inner-German flights.
441	Bonn tel 720 WRL 021/6	12 July	Reports US unwillingness to give even tacit agreement to inner-German flights.
442	Bonn tel 782 MRA 184/623/1	8 Aug	Expresses allied concern lest Berlin *Senat's* proposal to cut air services threaten freedom of manœuvre.
443	Bonn tel 895 WRL 184/1	19 Sept	Reports provisional agreement on winter schedules for Berlin air services.
444	Tel 559 to Bonn WRL 184/1	27 Sept	Welcomes news in No. 443.
445	Letter: Mallaby to Synnott WRL 184/1	28 Nov	Summarises current position on Berlin aviation.
446	Bonn tel 1162 MRA 184/623/1	29 Nov	Recommends agreement to new inner-German air services, while making clear disquiet at lack of consultation.
447	Bonn tel 1200 WRL 184/1	7 Dec	Reports that Americans propose discussion of aviation issues at forthcoming meeting of Political Directors in Brussels.

448	Bonn tel 1201 WRL 184/1	7 Dec	Transmits text of allied 'talking points' proposed by Americans.
449	Letter: Moss to Synnott MRA 184/623/1	10 Dec	Comments on No. 445: allied carriers could not be expected to maintain air services without limits on activities of inner-German carriers.
450	Letter: Broomfield to Synnott WRL 184/1	14 Dec	Assesses GDR's likely reaction to points raised in No. 445.
451	BMG Berlin tel 94 WRL 921/2	20 Dec	Reports Momper's desire for talks on the Berlin initiative to be pursued as quickly as possible.
452	Memorandum by WED WRL 184/1	21 Dec	Examines options regarding Berlin and inner-German air services.
453	Bonn tel 11 WRL 184/1	**1990** 5 Jan	Argues that allies should take the lead in presenting their aviation concept to the Germans.
454	Minute: Synnott to Ratford WRL 184/1	7 Feb	Briefs on rationale behind UK line on Berlin aviation.
455	Bonn tel 163 WRL 184/1	8 Feb	Reports joint allied presentation on aviation to FRG.
456	Letter: Neville-Jones to Weston WRL 184/1	9 Feb	Sets out allied negotiating tactics for next round of talks on aviation.
457	Minute: Wordsworth to Ratford WRL 184/1	21 Feb	Briefs on forthcoming meeting on Berlin air services: UK negotiating position would not be improved by blocking FRG/GDR flights.
458	Bonn tel 384 WRL 184/1	23 Mar	Reports on discussion between allied and FRG representatives of proposals for inner-German services.
459	Minute: Synnott to Weston DZN 061/97	25 Apr	Summarises situation as Western allies approach Russians to secure practical improvements in Berlin aviation.
460	BMG Berlin tel 37 to Bonn ESC 020/36	21 May	Reports Soviet wish to pursue aviation issue in context of talks on German unification.

Security Issues, February-September 1990

The hurried pace of German unification and prevailing uncertainties with regard to Soviet intentions spurred British officials into reconsidering the future of the allied military presence in Berlin. Burton felt that the Western powers might want to remain temporarily in Berlin after the city's incorporation in a united Germany. In a telegram of 19 February 1990 he suggested that four-power rights over Berlin should be separated from those in relation to Germany as a whole and that they might prolong certain aspects of them, such as the right to maintain military forces there. Substantial Soviet forces still remained between Berlin and the Elbe and Burton did not want Berlin to be left hostage to Soviet unpredictability. However, he contended, the maintenance of forces would have to be by agreement with the Germans for an indefinite period until a degree of stability had been reached and four-power rights were no longer required (No. 461). Other officials were not so sure: 'do we', asked Simon Hemans of the Soviet Department, 'or the Germans, or indeed the Russians, really want to retain them [allied rights] in the longer term?' Would they not, he added, 'serve as a mute reminder of Soviet failure and Soviet inability to prevent a situation which overwhelmed them' (No. 462)? Munro was also convinced HMG should aim to bring the British presence in Berlin into line with that in the FRG by replacing rights based on conquest with agreements negotiated with Germany. He thought that if Soviet forces were going to intervene in politics anywhere it would be in the Soviet Union, not Germany. And in a letter to Hilary Synnott of the Western European Department he sounded a cautionary note: 'if the Germans gained the impression that we were seeking to maintain a military presence in Berlin sustained by Allied rights ... they would soon regard us as unpredictable, dangerous, and hostile to German unity' (No. 465). Burton was persuaded to accept that the firm position adopted by the Federal Government as well as the Berlin *Senat*, and a US disinclination to take a contrary view, made it unlikely that any existing allied rights could be retained. Yet he remained concerned about the potential threat posed by Soviet troops in East Germany to Berlin's security. Moreover, he insisted that, if, as seemed probable, the Germans were to request the continuance of an allied presence in Berlin, the British would need to be very clear what they were being asked to do 'and whether it [was] really in [their] interest to do it on those terms' (No. 466).

The West Germans were willing to negotiate, and in a message to Thatcher of 17 July 1990 Kohl formally requested the maintenance of a British presence in Berlin for so long as Soviet forces remained in Germany (No. 480). But, as was pointed out in an FCO paper on the future of allied garrisons in Berlin, more was at stake than the future security of the city. Their presence, the paper argued, would 'permit the continuation of our intelligence effort in Berlin; this provides an insight into the Soviet military which we should continue to exploit as long as the target remains'. They could also be used 'as a bargaining counter, to be withdrawn at the end of the transitional period in exchange for the withdrawal of Soviet troops from former East German territory' (No. 481). Documents pertaining to these issues and the subsequent discussions are included in this group.

DOCUMENT SUMMARIES

	DOCUMENT	DATE	MAIN SUBJECT
461	BM Berlin tel 24 WRL 012/1	**1990** 19 Feb	Considers future of allied military presence in Berlin in the light of German unification.
462	Minute: Hemans to	20 Feb	Argues that it would be

	Synnott ESC 020/36		'inconceivable' that Soviet Union would use force to hang on to, or in, Berlin.
463	Special Order of the Day by British Commandant, Berlin WRL 400/1	20 Feb	Announces that no decision had yet been taken to reduce the garrison.
464	Bonn tel 225 WRL 012/1	21 Feb	Reports that FRG was unlikely to be willing to allow garrisons to remain in Berlin on the basis of allied 'residual rights'.
465	Letter: Munro to Synnott WRL 012/1	23 Feb	Argues that HMG 'must be prepared to give up the rights we acquired by conquest and replace them with agreements'.
466	Letter: Burton to Synnott WRL 012/1	6 Mar	Contends that presence of allied troops in Berlin was not necessarily in either allied or UK interest.
467	Teleletter: Burton to Mallaby DZN 061/97	20 Mar	Expands on No. 466 in relation to security framework in which allied troops might remain in Berlin.
468	Bonn tel 378 WRL 012/1	23 Mar	Maintains that if allied forces were to remain in Berlin 'this should be at explicit German request'.
469	Letter: Eyers to Synnott WRL 012/1	23 Mar	Argues that Burton was advocating a high-risk strategy, and Germans should not be forced into position of *demandeurs*.
470	BM Berlin tel 6 DZN 061/97	27 Mar	Reports Defence Secretary's meeting with Momper on British troops in Berlin: 'we would stay as long as we were wanted and needed'.
471	Minute: Synnott to Lever WRL 012/1/90	4 Apr	Reviews key military and political considerations for Berlin 'end-game'.
472	Minute: Lever to Synnott DZN 061/97	9 Apr	Responds to No. 471: stresses need for agreed allied line.
473	BM Berlin tel 20 to Bonn ESC 020/36	20 Apr	Reports non-committal Soviet response to Western *démarche* on opening of border crossings to allied personnel.
474	Minute: Synnott to Wall WRL 040/1	13 June	Contends that there was nothing to be gained from opposing US wishes to celebrate closure of Checkpoint Charlie.
475	BM Berlin tel 47	22 June	Reports Checkpoint Charlie

	WRL 040/1		closure ceremony and Shevardnadze's proposal for withdrawal of forces.
476	BM Berlin tel 55 to Bonn DZN 061/97	25 June	Reports that *Senat* thought a complete withdrawal of forces from Berlin could only follow departure of Soviet troops from East Germany.
477	Letter: Mallaby to Weston WRL 012/1	28 June	Reviews current thinking on the future of the Berlin garrison.
478	Minute: Hedley to DUS(P), MOD WRL 012/1	4 July	Reports on visit to Berlin and matters relating to the garrison.
479	BM Berlin tel 53 DZN 061/97	20 July	Considers questions to be addressed before responding to FRG request for retention of Western forces in Berlin.
480	Minute: Synnott to Broomfield DZN 061/97	20 July	Submits draft reply from Thatcher to Kohl, agreeing to maintenance of a British military presence in Berlin while Soviet troops remain in East Germany.
481	Letter: Weston to Neville-Jones DZN 061/97	24 July	Refers to No. 477 and encloses paper setting out considerations relating to future of allied garrisons in Berlin.
482	Letter: Powell to Gozney DZN 061/97	25 July	Transmits final text of Thatcher's message to Kohl about allied garrisons in Berlin.
483	Tel 1315 to Washington DZN 061/97	26 July	Instructs Ambassadors in Washington and Paris to sound out host governments on their responses to request for allied troops to remain in Berlin.
484	Paris tel 854 DZN 061/97	27 July	Informs that French thinking was 'not as developed as ours' on Berlin garrison.
485	Washington tel 1770 DZN 061/97	27 July	Reports that State Department shares HMG's concerns and welcomes consultation on Berlin.
486	Letter: Neville-Jones to Weston DZN 061/97	17 Aug	Summarises 'state of the debate in Bonn' on the future of the Berlin garrison.
487	Minute: Goulden to Ricketts DZN 061/97	21 Aug	Comments on No. 486: 'we will need flexibility if we are to reach agreed arrangements with the Germans instead of simply being bounced'.
488	Bonn tel 1073 DZN 061/97	27 Aug	Asserts need to plan suitable public event to mark end of the

			allied role and departure of Commandants on 3 October.
489	Tel 574 to Bonn DZN 061/97	3 Sept	Responds positively to No. 488.

Berlin: Status and Allied Rights, November 1989-October 1990

In the late autumn of 1989 British diplomats were still uncertain about Germany's future and therefore about Britain's position in Berlin. In a letter to Synnott of 30 November Mallaby acknowledged that the threat to West Berlin had 'receded greatly'. But, he added, it had 'not disappeared'. 'The situation in the GDR', he observed, 'is unstable and instability there and/or in other parts of Eastern Europe may last years.' And while he assumed that the Western allies could not stay in Berlin if the Berliners did not want them there, he thought they had an interest in staying so long as the German question was not settled, for their presence symbolised their 'right to a say in the answer to that question' (No. 491). As, however, the documents in this group indicate, the status of Berlin and the role of the occupying powers there were challenged by day-to-day developments in the city and the GDR. Mallaby thought there was likely to be particular pressure in four areas: aviation, the relationship between the Western sectors and the FRG, East Berlin, and the Quadripartite Agreement. The Western allies might seek, as in the past, to preserve the special legal status of Berlin under four-power occupation, but they had increasingly to accept the *de facto* trend of the greater integration of the Western sectors into the FRG (No. 492). They had also, as Synnott suggested in his reply to Mallaby, to maintain their military preparedness 'in case the present welcome trend of reforms in the Soviet Union and Eastern Europe more generally were to prove unsustainable' (No. 494). Meanwhile, consideration was given to how to react both to proposals for West Berlin's participation in direct elections to the *Bundestag*, and to speculation that the Russians might want to return to the allied *Kommandatura* (Nos. 493 & 496-98).

Thatcher, though not ready to stand out against the FRG's aspirations regarding Berlin, did 'not want to rail-road the Russians into agreeing' to direct elections, and thought the best course 'to try to lie low ... until the Russians show[ed] their hand' (No. 497). Yet on 6 June 1990, at a meeting of NATO Foreign Ministers at Turnberry in Ayrshire, it was agreed that the Western allies would lift their reservation preventing Berliners from directly electing the *Bundestag* and denying Berlin representatives in the two houses of the Federal German parliament full voting rights (No. 501). The holding of free local elections in East Berlin likewise weakened the basis of further FCO opposition to contacts between British officials and the municipal authorities there. British diplomats recognised that 'the legal and factual situations [had] diverged' (No. 502). Donald Lamont, Counsellor in the British Mission, Berlin, the renamed BMG, felt that the gap between the date of German reunification and the termination of allied rights could be particularly awkward: 'there could', he noted, 'be a negative reaction from the Berlin population if signs of allied authority remained after reunification' (No. 500). Consequently, at midnight on 2 October 1990, four-power rights and responsibilities for Germany as a whole and Berlin were suspended in unison. The following day the British Commandant left Berlin. As Mallaby concluded, Berlin was now 'no longer an island of freedom in a sea of oppression but the largest city and the nominal capital of a united Germany'. Nevertheless, the story was not quite over: the Berliners wanted the Western allied garrisons to stay until Soviet forces fulfilled their commitment to depart Germany by the end of 1994 (No. 507).

DOCUMENT SUMMARIES

	DOCUMENT	DATE	MAIN SUBJECT
490	Letter: Burton to Mallaby WRL 370/3	**1989** 14 Nov	Advises on strategy towards the 'endgame' in Berlin: sees opportunity for Britain to play an important role in new situation.
491	Letter: Mallaby to Synnott WRL 370/3	30 Nov	Comments on No. 490, and uncertainties over when allied role would end.
492	Bonn tel 1214 MRA 184/623/1	10 Dec	Reflects on current challenges to the status of Berlin.
493	Bonn tel 1215 WRL 020/8	10 Dec	Considers difficult issues raised by *Senat*'s wish for Berliners to elect representatives directly to *Bundestag*.
494	Letter: Synnott to Mallaby WRL 370/3	15 Dec	Insists that military preparedness should be maintained in case trend of reforms in Eastern Europe proves unsustainable.
495	Minute: Synnott to Brewer WRL 012/1	**1990** 29 Jan	Submits package of Berlin issues on which Allies must take decisions.
496	Letter: Gozney to Powell WRL 011/2	29 Jan	Discusses presentational, legal and political aspects of Berliners' representation in Bonn.
497	Letter: Powell to Gozney WRL 011/2	30 Jan	Replies to No. 496: Thatcher favours lying low on this issue 'until the Russians show their hand'.
498	Letter: Charlton to Dinwiddy WRL 020/3	9 Feb	Speculates on what might happen if Russians return to allied *Kommandatura*: potential dilemma for Western allies.
499	Letter: Grainger to Carter WRL 012/1	17 May	Lists Berlin issues to which Quadripartite Rights are attached, and which would need to be covered in any settlement.
500	Teleletter: Lamont to Synnott DZN 061/97	7 June	Argues that termination of Four Power Rights in Berlin should be at same time as, or close to, unification to avoid difficulties.
501	Minute: Synnott to Gozney	7 June	Submits (*a*) draft letter to No. 10 informing PM that allied Foreign

	WRL 011/2		Ministers have agreed to lift their reservation preventing Berliners' representation in Bonn; and (*b*) agreed draft letter to Kohl.
502	Letter: Synnott to Ramsden WRL 012/1	11 June	Agrees that in changed Berlin situation, there would be no objection to establishing working contacts with East Berlin municipal authorities.
503	Minute: Synnott to Weston WRL 012/1C	21 June	Suggests line to take in response to GDR proposal for immediate abolition of QRR in Berlin: dangers of 'à la carte' approach.
504	Letter: Grainger to Salvesen WRL 012/1	2 July	Refers to No. 503 and discusses points for negotiation with Soviet Union.
505	Despatch: Burton to Mallaby WRL 012/1	2 Oct	Assesses British and allied achievement in Berlin: opening of Wall was 'a vindication of all we had stood for'.
506	Teleletter: Burton to Mallaby WRL 012/1	5 Oct	Reports on unification ceremonies and tributes on 2-3 Oct: 'The Berlin endgame ended on a high note for the Allies'.
507	Despt: Mallaby to Hurd WRL 012/1	10 Oct	Transmits No. 505: 'Berlin is no longer an island of freedom in a sea of oppression but the largest city and the nominal capital of united Germany.'
508	Letter: Synnott to Mallaby WRL 012/1	19 Nov	Comments on Nos. 505 & 506.
509	Letter: Greenstock to Burton WRL 012/1	19 Nov	Conveys Hurd's appreciation of the work done by British Mission in Berlin during 'a unique period of diplomacy'.